THE PARAMETERS OF TRADITIONAL NUÄÄR MARRIAGE

By dr. James Mabor Gatkuoth

A Note from the Publisher

The publisher wishes to acknowledge and thank Dr Douglas H. Johnson for his invaluable help and support for Africa World Books and its mission of preserving and promoting African cultural and literary traditions and history. Dr Johnson and fellow historians have been instrumental in ensuring that African people remain connected to their past and their identity. Africa World Books is proud to carry on this mission.

© *Dr. James Mabor Gatkuoth*, 2021

ISBN: 978-0-6453010-1-4

All rights reserved.

No part of this publication may be reproduced, stored in a retrieval system, or transmitted, in any form, or by any means, electronic, mechanical, photocopying, recording or otherwise, without the prior permission of the publishers.

This book is sold subject to the conditions that it shall not, by way of trade or otherwise, be lent, re-sold, hired out or otherwise circulated without the publisher's prior consent in any form of binding or cover other than in which it is published and without a similar condition including the condition being imposed on the subsequent purchaser.

Cover design, typesetting and layout : Africa World Books

Dedication

This work is dedicated to all the Nuäär elders (some of whom I have acknowledged) who contributed and to the Nuäär emerging generations who deserve to know and perhaps acknowledge how their forefathers and ancestors organized the society they now inherit and enjoy which hopefully they shall pass on to their siblings.

Contents

Acknowledgements	xi
Introductory Background	1

Chapter One: The Marriage

Introduction	11
I. Conventional (common) *Nuäär* marital unions	14
1. Monogamy	14
2. Polygamy	16
3. Ghost Marriage	18
4. Child Marriages: Early Engagement of Spouse	19
5. Woman-to-Woman Marriages	19
6. Concubinage	21
7. Levirate Marriage: *Kueŋ ciek jɔkä duel*	22
8. Other peculiar Marriages	24
a. Marriage of Twins	24
b. Marriage of Monorchid *Tor*	25
c. Marriage of Deficient Persons	26
d. The Marriage Procedures of an Adopted Person	27

II. Sanctioned (barred) marriages among the *Nuäär*   28
1. Incest taboos   29
2. Unincestuous but selected taboo-associated marriages   30
3. People sharing a totem do not marry   31
4. Relations: *mar*   32
The end of *mar* relations   32
5. Marriage between age-mates and their children   33
    a. When to and not to marry *nyaricädu* age-mate's daughter   34
    b. Dropping out from an age-set to another   34
6. Other social factors for family integrity   36
    a. Divorce: *Dägh*   37
    b. Adultery: *Dhom*   38
    c. Attempted suicide: *Ɖaph*   38
    d. Gossip: *Löm*   39
    e. Thievery: *Kual*   39
    f. Evil-eye: *Pëth/Pɛdh*   39
    g. Red mouth: *ŋart*   40
7. Feud/homicide   40
8. Homicides not bars to marriage   42
    a. A husband killed by his wife   42
    b. Baby killed by sitter   42
    c. A pregnant woman raped and miscarriages   42
    d. Accidents   43

Chapter Two: The Evolution of Nuäär Family
Introduction   44
I. The Transition Stage   46
    a. Scarification/marking (*gäri*)   47
    b. The conduct/behaviour of a marked person   52
II. *Nuäär* marriage preliminaries   55

a. *Käm tuac*- civet cat skin giving either normally or conditionally. Once that is done he becomes a *kuud* whose behavior should be pleasing ... 60
Behaviour of a "*kuud*" ... 63
b. Selection and scrutiny of a spouse ... 65
Consensus on spouse choice ... 69
c. *Läär kuen*. Declaration of marriage ... 69
d. *Läär cieŋ* and scrutiny of the *kuud* ... 72
 (i) More suitors to marry ... 73
 (ii) The girl's family receives and screens the suitors ... 73
e. *Läär nhok*- confession or return of love, i.e Marriage is acceptable to the big people at home ... 76
f. *Luɔm nyal* ... 78
III. Rituals, festivals and ceremonies ... 79

Chapter Three: The Marriage Consummation Procedures
Marriage Procedures ... 85
 a. Booking the girl- *luɔm nyal*, the initial and formal marriage commitment ... 85
 b. *Paph yiyni* or *Määdni tuaini*. In-laws Joint Council Meeting ... 87
 c. *Cuɛc* betrothal the driving to the girl's home the first installment of bride-wealth ... 91
 d. Marriage or bride wealth negotiations: *Tuɔc* ... 97
 e. *Buɔr* ... 106
 f. *Luɔny tuaini* removal of civet cat skins ... 109
 (i) Significance of *luɔny tuaini* civet cat skins removal ... 109
 (ii) *Yaŋ buɔr* ... 110
 (iii) Details of bride-wealth collection ... 111
 g. *Muɔt nyal* Taking the bride. ... 111

h. *Ruy yɔa (Yaat)*. Dressing the woman with skin skirts. 117
  (i) *Yaŋ muɔt* 118
  (ii) Advices and safeguards to the newlywed couple. 120
i. *Dɔnyni cioyni ciek.* Stepping on the feet of the woman 125
j. *Ba nyal wicdɛ luɔc jɔk. Mään-* womanhood stage: a step before she cooks 128
II. Other condensed versions of *Nuäär* marriage stages 129
  a. The Nasir Version 129
    (i) *Noŋ and Muɔt Nyal* 136
    (ii) *Nuäär* Nasir marriage entitlements 137
  b. The *Gawäär* Version of *Nuäär* marriage 138
    (i) *Määtni tuaini* 142
    (ii) *Buɔr* 142
    (iii) *Luɔny tuaini* 143
    (iv) *Tuɔc* 144
    (v) *Muɔt nyal* 145
    (vi) *Cuŋ Kuen* Marriage rights/entitlements among the *Gawäär* 146

Chapter Four: Establishment of a Home
I. Housing 148
II. The bride's initial cooking: *That ciek* 151
III. Erection of household shrines. 157
  a. *Buɔr* 157
  b. *Riäk* altar 158
IV. *Dap ciek:* Birthing 160
V. Identification - Naming: *Ciot* 167
  a. Factors that influence naming a child 168
  b. Child naming 169
VI. Divorce or dissolution/termination of the marriage covenant 173

Chapter Five: Social Change in *Nuäär* Marriage 175
  I. War 176
  II. Displacement 178
  III. Migration- *Nuäär* in diaspora and the monetisation or
  dollarization of marriage 182
  IV. Christian Gospel 185

Summary and Conclusion
a. Summary 187
b. Conclusion 192

Appendices 195
Glossary 205
Bibliography 209
About the Author 211

Acknowledgments

This work owes its inspiration to Dr. Werner Daum - the former German Ambassador to the Sudan in late 1990's, and Prof. Simon Manoja, of the Anthropology Department, University of Juba, who recommended a direct approach to the Nuäär marriage. In regards to the substance, it is due to the following Nuäär people. (1)Thomas Tot Baŋɔaŋ, (2)Diu Kọk Warar, (3)Peter Yiedh Puɔk Mayian, (4) William Gai Caŋ, (5)Michael Mawic Macär, (6)Nyatik Kuɔl Kän, (7)Simon Can Kuɔr, (8)Clement Gattod Ɖundɛaŋ (died), (9)Peter Buoth Wuɔl (died), (10)Yoanis Tɛr Mɛt, (11)Jacob Rɛadh, (12) Abraham Cägh Riäk, (13)David Duɔb Puɔc, (14)John Wijial Kueth, (15)Gabriel Koŋ Chol, (16)Kɔaŋ Biɛl Kueth, (17)Thomson Thɔan Tɛny, (18)Mahmoud Ruɔt Kaŋ, (19)Michael Tɔi Jɔak (died), (20) Malɛk Duph, (21)Peter Taŋ Ɖundɛaŋ, (22)Kerubino Gatkek Liäy, (23)Peter Kuɔŋ Wei, (24)Dhil Gatluak Nyäk (died), (25)Zakaria Puɔk Riɛl Gatluak, (26)Kɔaŋ Thany Tɔi Tɛny, (27)Daniel Nen Nhial, (28)John Wejaŋ Machär, (29)Waŋ Mut Luɔny, (30)Yoanis Puɔk Kuic, (31)Joseph Tut Jɔak, (32)Nyakual Kɔy (died), (33)Peter Ɖuɛn Kọl, (34)Thomas Wijial Chɔap. (35)Rev. Michael Chɔt Lul, (36)Ezekiel Muɔn Kulaŋ (died), (37)Ruɔt Duɔl Rɛth, (38)Hon. Thomas Kumɛ Kän (died), (39)Thomas Tut Kọl, (40)David Thɔl

Dieu (41) Kuac Gatluak Badɛŋ (42) Gabriel Gany Tër, (43)Mrs. Nyadiaŋä Pan Dɛaŋ, (44) Mrs. Ann Nyabärciaŋ Macär, (45)Mrs. Mary Cöl Yɔŋ Thɔan, (46) Mrs Nyakiɛr Goloŋ Kon, (47) Mrs Cuɔi Gatäkuɔth Nyäk (48) Mr. Peter Zimzim Gatkuoth Dec, (49) Mr. Robert Ruai Makun who contributed his luak and cattle to be the image (cover) of this book and last but not least (50)Dr. John Gai Yɔɣ whose reflections on the matter refined some hanging issues. Therefore, they all deserve my gratitude for the information each offered to me during the initial and the last stages of this research. It is lamentable that some died before they could see the effect of their input to this work. However, with them we have tried to give whatever we could remember of the Nuäär culture on marriage. But I stand alone for any errors and other shortcomings/mistakes.

Above all I can't forget to thank my dear wife - Alice James Akoth- (aca Kɔi Nhial or Kɔi Nyayɔaŋ), who continuously pressed on me to finish this undertaking. The entire family had to put up with the many long inconvenient interviews conducted at home that resulted in their neglect. I appreciate their endurance of the tedious hours spent in sitting, transcribing the interviews and writing. Hopefully, they will recognize the fruit of their suffering for this research.

Introductory Background on *Nuäär* (Naath) and Their Marriage

The *Nuäär*, who also call themselves nɛi ti naadh Naath[1], are Nilotic people who are considered population-wise, the second-largest nationality in South Sudan. At the beginning of the 19th century, they started to migrate from Liic in Western *Nuäär* land (present Unity State) eastwards across the Nile and Zeraf rivers pushing further into Western Ethiopia. They are agro-pastoralists who seem to balance subsistence agriculture with cattle herding. However, they do fishing and wildlife hunting, as well.

The *Nuäär* people are a federation of sections and clans that now dominate Bentiu (former Western Upper Nile), Fan-gak and Akobo (Central *Nuäär*), and Nasir (Eastern *Nuäär*). River Nile is the principal geographical dividing line in addition to the Zeraf stream and the Sobat River. Most of the *Nuäär* homeland is located in the swamp areas. It is imbued with enormous deposits of petroleum and other natural resource potential including wildlife, fisheries, acacia senegalese (gum arabica), and balantines aegyptiucm (laloob).

The *Nuäär* that were dislodged by the war of 1983-2005 and

---

1   *Naath* means people. *Nei ti Naath-* the actual humanbeings. Raan is single while naath is plural.

that of 2013 to date, have become South Sudanese refugees in the diaspora. They formed significant communities in Omaha, Nebraska, the United States of America and in Australia and speak the same Thök Naath language. The various dialects that the *Ethnologue* has listed are spoken by all the *Nuäär* communities-Jikäny(*cieŋ* and dɔar-western and eastern), Lɔu, Nyuɔŋ, *Thiaŋ*, Bul Chol Geay, Gawaar, Jagɛi (gë kɔac), Laak, Leek (nyääl), Dok Guë and Gatbä*kol*-Kuoth.

Apart from the binding language indicated above, there are cultural prescriptions and proscriptions that organize life and relationship among the *Nuäär*. Marriage is one of the cultural traits that has social significance for the perpetuation of life. *Nuäär* cultural values and attitudes are transmitted to successive generations through the family. Accordingly, to marry and be married is a right that no *Nuäär* should be deprived of. Normal *Nuäär* marriage is the male choice of a spouse which is arranged, guided and consensual. No *Nuäär* girl of marriageable age is ever asked to get married. She has three stages to pass through: she is a *pith* growing, then *guar*-halfway to marriage and then jut. At this last stage of *jut*, she is mature enough to be married. She has to be provided with ornaments to be fully a *kuud* i.e. about to be married. The spouse choice and the payment of bride-wealth are the two important aspects of *Nuäär* marriage. Spouse choice starts with *käm tuac* the young man being offered a civet cat skin to wear as a license to marry. The payment of bride-wealth is based on the concept of *ciek ɛ ciek cieŋ* (family wife) "wife belongs to the family". These two concepts *käm tuac*- the offering of civet cat skin and family wife *ciek ɛ ciek cieŋ,* make the *Nuäär* marriage to be supported and praised. The marriage then unites the *cieŋ* families/clan, tribe and the community at large. It is because of this significance that any problems surrounding the marriage urgently concern the whole family or the clan.

Relationships are based on a cohesive family unit (all the brothers and sisters and their own children), friends, the neighbourhood, the village, and perhaps the linguistic group. Along with the family, the outside community exercises considerable control and authority over individual attitudes and behaviour. *Nuäär* families, households and clans are collectively responsible for the marriage of their sons and daughters. Their marital relationship does not end as long as it had occurred. The married girl is usually likened to a wet land or rich riverian grazing area '*töc*'[2] because what the in-laws get in turn is much more than the cattle entitlements. The *Nuäär* people say that "even if all the cattle claims have been paid to the bride's relatives, the real marriage is one thousand cattle". The father-in-law and the other in-laws take something at a time. They keep feeding on their daughter as an endless loan.

Marriage among the *Nuäär* is a right that is directly connected with the perpetuation of the family genealogical tree. Therefore, no *Nuäär* should ever be deprived of it. Families, households and clans have an obligation to procure at least one wife for a male and ensure that their daughters are married in any case. Since a married woman belongs to the household *ciek ε ciek cieŋ*, all the relatives participate in her choice and scrutiny, in cattle payment to procure her and in the celebrations. *Nuäär* culture restricts marriage to people outside the extended circle of kin. By kinship extension, no *Nuäär* people of the same ancestral origin, sharing totem, age-mates, or blood relatives within five (female side) to six generations (male side) are allowed to marry or even have sexual relations. *Nuäär* are bound by incest prohibitions, bride-wealth entitlements and their concept of woman or female belonging to nowhere, to prefer marriage everywhere outside the kinship circle. The *Nuäär* prefer that a wife is obtained by negotiations and payment of a bride-wealth.

---

2   'Töc' is a swamp wherein fish and water foods are got apart from the grazing opportunities for the herd.

Nuäär marriage is a series of events in a chronological sequence. That chronological order provides the organizational structure for the process. The order is simply followed as instructions to aspirants for performing the marriage. *Kuen* marriage to *Nuäär* is not merely the acquisition of a wife but having counted and paid cattle or properties convertible to cattle for a wife. A married woman must necessarily have incurred her husband's cattle payment. The *Nuäär* believe that marriage enhances one's influence within the community because of the in-laws and other people. So, a *Nuäär* man would prefer to offer his daughters to, or make his sons marry from well-known families. Marriage is therefore useful in forming social alliances that enable people to consolidate in bands of a strong fighting force. Because pastoral societies are highly mobile and competitive, they need these bands to withstand attacks from others. As an alliance between family groups, marriage is arranged by family heads in order to cement social relationships between different kinship groups. The success or failure of marriage then becomes a concern to the couple and the whole society.

There is a *Nuäär* saying that "if one missed marriage, it was bet-ter not to have been created."[3] Missing marriage in this context is having chosen a bad woman. Among the Bentiu *Nuäär* of the Unity State in South Sudan, people regret the cattle paid towards a bad marriage and wish they were for homicide.[4] So marriage is very important because children would be born. Rising from death in Christianity would mean to *Nuäär* that one has children. The happiest day for a parent is the wedding of a son or a daughter. *Nuäär* do not accredit an unmarried person with authority such as chieftainship or leadership which are reserved for married men. A

---

3   *Ciek me wut pany-* a sermon by Rev. Michael Chɔt Lul during the marriage of daughter of David Thɔl Dieu, October 24, 2002-   Omdurman.
4   This was according to Zakaria Puɔk Riɛl Gat*luak* who was interviewed in Jebra May 2005.

family or house without a wife is an incomplete one, just as a man without a wife is half human to *Nuäär*. At least if one had married one wife, he is relieved from becoming a *thuɔm-* ghost.

Although the functions served by marriage vary from one society to another, the *Nuäär* prize and value it as an important life goal between males and females. Most *Nuäär* couples enter marriage hoping to enjoy a life-long and loving partnership blessed with children. Marriage is a means of recruiting new members to a line of descent. Marriage is a serious concern to many people than the spouses themselves. It has rules and ceremonies. A *Nuäär* man marries to have a name to be remembered or talked about. It is independence for the ŋuɛat young man. He establishes *tuac/ruay*[5] relationships through the marriage. Marriage is still considered first as the covenant between two individual families and then clans. It is a publicly announced legitimate sexual union. The marriage bond ties the two individuals together. It also spells out their reciprocal rights and obligations towards one another and their children. The social structure is organised around the family.[6]

Marriage is one custom that moves people from one status to another. The wedding rituals socially provide entertainment and excitement for the participants from society. They serve as public announcements for the people to know the newly wedded bride and groom. In turn, the community participants have to support and recognize the man and the woman being married. The couple is then advised to learn the community values, commitments and ethical ideals pertaining to their new roles.

Some scholars-notably Evans-Pritchard, Raymond C. Kelly, Sharon Hutchinson and others that I had no chance to access their

---

5   *Tuac* is in-laws and ruay is an old word for in-laws too. It is the civet cat skin that symbolizes this relationship.
6   Paul G. Hierbert, Cultural Anthropology, BakerBook House, Grand Rapids, Michigan 49506, 1983. p. 166

writings, have worked out commendable information on the main units of *Nuäär* marriage. I have no reason to delve into them except to commend them for exposing the *Nuäär* culture. For instance, in his writing about "Kinship and Marriage Among the *Nuer*" (sic), Evans-Pritchard chose to explain the way in which social life is maintained and carried forward. He dwelt on the internal factors that make the social system continue. Some discussion is devoted on *Nuäär* marriage as a series of unions forming a network of kinship ties. He highlighted prohibitions, incest, and the various forms of marriage including concubinage. He described how the marriage is brought about commencing with *läär cieŋ* betrothal, *ŋut* the wedding and the *mut* consummation as the chief of ceremonies. Also included are courtship, ceremonies, payment of bride-wealth, birthing, codes of behaviour etc. The additional new consideration involves details, certain important steps skipped and the assertion that *nyadhuɔri* is the ideal marriage among the *Nuäär*. Other unions are not considered marriages because they are not ritualised.

The book "The *Nuer* Conquest" by Raymond C. Kelly, emphasized that the importance of marriage to *Nuäär* is reflected in their obligation to pay cattle to acquire a wife even for a dead brother (ghost, spirit). Hence the *Nuäär* expeditions for land and cattle acquisition were forced on them by the desirability of polygamy and the obligation to provide a wife for a deceased kinsman.

The quantity of animals (cattle, sheep, goats) negotiated and agreed upon by both parents of the bride and groom, in the marriage discussions, is to be transferred as the bride-wealth. Raymond investigated the size of bride-wealth payments and noted that the "ideal" and "acceptable" rate delineated by each *Nuäär* tribe was based on the customary claims, expectations of the bride's kin, and the circumstances of the groom's kin. It will be found that this third condition is not considered because no one ever brings it up in the discussions. The groom's people cannot say they have no cows yet are interested in that lady. Certainly, she won't be given out for free. Among the prohibitions documented by Raymond are that a man should not marry from his own clan or from those genealogically related to him through a common antecedent. This is strictly tied to cattle rights, which, according to their rotation, keep diminishing from a cow to a mere spear and then nothing.

Sharon Hutchinson ar*gued* in "The *Nuer* Dilemmas" that *Nuäär* are "no longer the isolated, independent, cattle-minded warriors immortalized by Evans-Pritchard..."[7] *Nuäär* people are trying to cope up with the contemporary challenges that seem to undermine their traditional set-up. The transformations imposed on them date to the British colonial rule, followed by the stability enjoyed during the autonomy period for the South Sudan between 1972-1983; the impact of the civil wars 1955-72 and 1983- 2003. These factors have put *Nuäär* in a dilemma where they "struggle to comprehend and come to terms with the massive social and economic transformations wrought (by those factors)..."[8] Sharon also focused on incest as a bar to marriage with other taboo-associated prohibitions.

Those scholarly works are short of some detailed description and explanation of many other steps in the *Nuäär* marriage. For an in-depth understanding of the *Nuäär* marriage conventions and procedures, this work provides additional considerations that were skipped in the previous studies. On the whole, the effort is expected to answer such questions like who to marry? What is bride-wealth? Is *Nuäär* marriage exogamic or endogamic? The details of ceremonies should specify who sacrifices what and on which occasion, with details of the prayers. Are the names of the

---

7   Sharon E.Hutchinson, The *Nuer* Dilemmas, University of California Press, Berkeley, Los Angeles, London, 1996. p. 25.
8   Sharon Ibid., p.27.

children related to the father, mother and their kin? These important details and some steps were skipped particularly the assertion that the ideal marriage among the *Nuäär* is that of *nyadhuɔri* or that of *kea* for a poor man. Other unions not ritualised are not considered marriages. The importance of marriage is reflected in the sixteen steps that must be followed and implemented accordingly. The rationale behind each step deserves to be described and explained in detail. It is the most important reference point in the transition process to adulthood. This is done with a background that the *Nuäär* society has prescriptions and proscriptions, which provide order and security for its people. The collectivity of *Nuäär* marriage is clear both in decision-making, in festivities and the attendant obligations. In these ceremonies, all the members of the family- be they the departed, the living, or yet to be born, must be involved directly or indirectly.

Much of the material is from the researcher's personal involvement in and observation of marriages, and from interviews conducted on a sample of 50 individuals (including 7 women), both old and young people, from the different *Nuäär* tribal sections. This work narrates the parameters of traditional (not time-bound) *Nuäär* marriage particularly the rites and associated social practices that *Nuäär* think are a window into understanding the dynamics of the *Nuäär* culture and their entire society. If the *Nuäär* marriage process is viewed from how new families are forged, expanded and differentiated, this will reveal how *Nuäär* broad relations of mutual dependence and independence are formed, balanced and transformed. I think such insight into the marriage processes, rites and other surrounding expectations is important for whoever is interested and wants to know, compare and contrast the *Nuäär* marriage then and now. This work is laid out in five short chapters. There is an introductory background on the *Nuäär* people, their customs, traditions and their right to marry, marriage functions/ conditions, and rituals. The first chapter deals with the types of marriage preferable to *Nuäär* and the rationale behind the bars that limit, dictate or prescribe the choice of the type of marriage. This is expected to answer questions such as: Who can marry without hinderances? What are the preferred marriages? Who initiates the marriage? What steps are necessary for its culmination into contract and what steps could be skipped? Chapter two is on the evolution of *Nuäär* family particularly the transitional stages, *Nuäär* marriage preliminaries and the rituals, festivals and ceremonies associated with the marriage. The third chapter concentrates on the marriage consummation procedures and other condensed marriage versions from other *Nuäär* clans. Chapter four focuses on the establishment of a home that entails building an abode, woman's cooking, shrine construction, birthing and naming of a new child and if marriage can elapse or not. The social change in *Nuäär* marriage due to the impact of war, displacement, migration (*Nuäär* in diaspora), and the Christian gospel is briefly explored in chapter five. A summary of the main features of *Nuäär* marriage and a conclusion wind-up the whole research.

CHAPTER ONE
The Marriage

Introduction

Every culture, or ethnic group, has its own unique traditions regarding marriage and the wedding ceremony. These diverse and varied traditions provide an insight into the conditions preset by each group at the time. However, societies differ in who, when, how and how many one may marry. Some societies forbid, encourage or require certain types of marriages. Other societies restrict the choice of, and specify, the potential marriage partners. The regulations and customs developed by the different cultures categorize the kin and other social identities between which marriage is prohibited, allowed, preferred and prescribed. Hence, marriage relationships are patterned on exogamy and endogamy.

Among the *Nuäär*, marriage is a right[9] and the wife belongs to the whole household. The right to marry and be married is associated

---

[9] This is fully covered by this author in another book- "*Nuäär* Social Rights and Obligations" published in 2012.

with the responsibility to sustain and perpetuate the race. At this stage, the family, clan and kinsmen have now the responsibility to fund his marriage. Since *Nuäär* marriage aims to expand the family circle of relatives with useful affines, it is considered eternal life because the offspring perpetuate the name of a person. These factors make *Nuäär* to marry for ghosts and inherit wives of deceased relatives. Accordingly, every *Nuäär* person- living or dead, normal or abnormal, is entitled to marry at least once. Hence, the common patterns of family making among the *Nuäär* are monogamy, exogamy, polygamy, polygyny, levirate (though not considered marriage), woman-to-woman marriage, ghost marriage and concubinage. The types of marriages listed above show that societal and cultural attitudes vary towards marriage. In fact, betrothal, arranged marriages, and marriage by individual choice are the different ways in which marriages are agreed upon. These marriages are concluded particularly according to the wishes of the couple and their lineages that work to extend their network of partners across the communities.

Mbiti emphatically put it that the right to marry is never compromised by Africans because "… marriage is a duty, a requirement from the corporate society and a rhythm of life in which everyone must participate. Otherwise, he who does not participate in it is a curse to the community, he is a rebel and a lawbreaker, he is not only abnormal but 'under human'. Failure to get married under normal circumstances means that the person concerned has rejected society and society rejects him in turn".[10]

Not to compromise this right to marry or be married, a young man from Western *Nuäär* Jikäny decided to have an incestuous case. He married his sister. His story runs like this:

---

10   Mbiti, John S., *African Religions and Philosophy,* London and Nairobi, Heinemann, 1969, p. 133.

A man married his sister because they were orphans. His sister was older and nobody wanted to marry her because their relatives were few and poor as they had no cattle. His sister was not married, they had no cattle and their only maternal uncle had males yet without cattle himself. He advised his sister that "We better do it and even if it will kill us, so be it". He slept with his sister who later gave birth to a baby boy. When the news spread that somebody married his own sister he was reported to the government (the native administration). The government opened a case against him. He and his wife with their son went to the town (Bentiu) for a court case. He asked who was suing him and was told it was the government. He asked the government if this was its daughter. This was positively answered. He challenged the government to relate the charge. Nobody could raise the issue. A certain old man, a spectator, told him "My son, just explain to them (assembled chiefs in court) what you have done for the first time in *Nuäär*land". He related his story thus: "My father and mother died. I have a maternal uncle who has boys without girls. My sister is older than me and nobody wants to marry her because we are a small clan. My sister and I realized that I shall not marry because I have no cows and my sister will not be married as she is also ageing. So, we thought if doing it will kill us, we care less. Accordingly, we decided to marry. This is what has happened". The chiefs were perplexed about how to judge it. The old man who asked him had to bless them that "Son of my brother, you will prosper". They remained a couple and continued to produce children normally.

I. Conventional (common) Nuäär marital unions
Throughout the world some of the recognized marriages are[11]

---

11   Mercy Amba Oduyoye & Musimbi R.A. Kanyoro (edit). The Will to Rise, Orbis Books, Maryknoll. NY.10545, 1992.[Oduyoye/Ko*nya*ro].p.121

(1) monogamy, (2) polygamy, (3) ghost marriage, (4) child marriage, woman-to-woman marriages, and (6) levirate. However, monogamy, polygamy and polyandry are some of the marriage contracts people use. But the version of marriage allowed may depend on the geographical location and the religious make-up of that society. Sometimes the availability of males and females, and the economic status of the society determine marriage. It seems strict monogamy-marriage between two people, is so far the form of marriage universally recognized and acceptable in most, if not, all societies. Some societies have serial monogamy, in which a person may marry more than once, so long as that person has only one spouse at a time.

Some societies practise exogamy that rules that a person must marry outside his cultural group. This is in line with the *Nuäär* concept that *Nyal* thilε wεi 'a girl has no definite land'. This means that the girl belongs to anywhere. She can be married outside the cultural group provided the *Nuäär* conditions for acquiring the bride are met.

As indicated that a *Nuäär* wife belongs to the household ε *ciek cieŋ*, all the family members have a say in her choice. In fact, the relatives do exercise an effective veto on marriage choice. Hence, *Nuäär* marriage may be assumed to be of convenience or expediency rather than of love. Actual love is built in the relationship at home as a family. It is never expressed except in songs of praise during dances and in other relevant or certain ceremonies.

1. Monogamy

The *Nuäär* society does not restrict on the number of wives nor put conditions about how they are to be treated. Therefore, one can acquire as many wives as he can afford to pay for or inherit customarily through ghost or levirate. However, a man may add to his house some concubines (covered below) who are not his wives in the full sense.

The practice of monogamy- taking of one wife, is always enforced. Monogamy that ends solitary life and begins a family tree is the most basic requirement among the *Nuäär*. It is widespread among the *Nuäär* as the minimum form of marital union. The relatives are obliged (in fact they should afford) to pay bride-wealth for at least the first (one) wife.

Since one wife is a right to start with, monogamy is the initial beginning of a family. Any *Nuäär* male who missed to marry for any reason, is considered a ghost. Hence, monogamy is relief from being considered a ghost. Eternal life to *Nuäär* tek in dorar[12] is marriage with children to maintain the family tree. *Nuäär* regard children as their real wealth and power. The marriage of a daughter is valued because it brings bride-wealth, which enables the family to acquire more livestock. The established relatives are a resort in times of need. In fact, *Nuäär* believe that "... a man with much livestock without wife or children is often regarded as poor".[13] Meanwhile, a man with many children and little livestock has high status and is often able to exercise great influence in community affairs. He can aspire for leadership as he is able to found a big lineage.

In the rural areas, many wives work in the fields to produce food for the household. Sufficient or surplus food resource is sometimes made into beer for casual visitors. Any person with such hospitality or service is usually congregated and accordingly establishes the winning of influence. If his female children are married once mature this extends his relations further through sons-in-law with

---

12   Life that sticks out without end. *Dor mi te rar.* A generation which is on earth.
13   Kɔaŋ Biɛl Kueth a 52-yr. old man from Tigjak people in Dok country. He was interviewed on August 4, 2001 in Khartoum.

their respective relatives. Therefore, through the female children one will absorb or enlist his sons-in-law for his protection or rescue, when the need arises. For the male children, other families would be attracted to this available manpower. They would marry from other families. Moreover, children are expected to help in the fields and gradually to join the labour force at the earliest age. In *Nuäär* society, whoever has the privilege of wealth or means to acquire that wealth can succeed to headmanship. The headmanship being a choice within the lineage, any aspirant can be voted in by his marriage alliances with different factions.

2. Polygamy
Within polygamy, there is polygyny which means that a man may have more than one wife. The other aspect is polyandry that stipulates multiple husbands i.e. a woman may have more than one husband. Polyandry is a kind of polygamy in which a woman has many husbands at a time i.e. a woman has multiple husbands at the same time. The practice of fraternal polyandry is common among Tibetans in Nepal, parts of China, parts of north India in which two or more brothers are married to the same woman and the wife has equal sexual access (arranged how?) to all of them. There would arise some difficulty in reconciling it with Article 16 of the United Nations document- UDHR. *Nuäär* would question or ask 'who chooses the wife among the brothers? Is consensus on the spouse sought and on whose initiative?' The *Nuäär* would hear it unusual for a woman to have several husbands who are incidentally brothers.

However, this practice is not in *Nuäär* society but is cited here for them (*Nuäär*) to know and note that other types of marriage have been researched and practiced in other parts of the world. This instance which permits a woman to have sexual relation with specified men other than her husband cannot be tolerated by *Nuäär*. In fact it is sanctioned by customary laws. *Nuäär* marriage is therefore polygynous. Among the *Nuäär*, the number of wives is dictated by one's status. To have more wives is a result of having properties with the intention of a large household. A young father with small children and enough cattle can marry. Older men have more wives through the resources they had accumulated over time and some wives inherited from their seniors. To ensure family cohesion that man has to state his elaborate rules for the precedence of wives and their children. This could even involve how their huts are to be placed in the layout of the homestead. He has to rank his children in marriage.

Although *Nuäär* believe that one wife can also create a big household, a *Nuäär* man would be proud to have multiple marriages or be married to many wives. With several wives, he is considered as a strong man with properties and big responsibilities. One other reason for polygamy is the fact that *Nuäär* fight a lot and kill each other but at the same time they want to maintain, if not increase, their manpower. Lest they are reduced they have to replenish the lost ones by multiple marriages. But to *Nuäär*, polyandry- the marriage of a woman to several husbands does not exist. It would be regarded a very severe sexual infidelity in that woman.[14] Instead if bride-wealth does not limit polygyny, *Nuäär* community women encourage polygyny for those husbands whose wives could not reproduce children, Sometimes the first wife may choose or induce her husband to take a junior wife. It is not uncommon for a wife to ask her husband to take another wife to help with the family duties, to have more children, or to add to her prestige as the dominant wife in a polygynous family.

---

14   Such a woman to *Nuäär* is a *ciek me ŋuan cɔu-* prostitute no less. She cannot be re-married.

3. Ghost Marriage

The institution of 'ghost marriage' was devised to cater for some ills within the *Nuäär* society. As indicated earlier many young men get killed in feuds or fights before they could marry. Even those who got married but were then killed are considered ghosts. Ghost and levirate marriages are not associated with the status of the man managing them because they are obligations rather than an addition to an individual husband.

In some cases, a woman may be married to the "ghost" of a man. The children she has by another man are attributed to the deceased to perpetuate his name. This is fictive marriage without biological but social husbands. Ghost marriages are a social intervention if a young man died before getting married. The family and clan get together and marry a wife in the name of the deceased. A close relative would be chosen to act as a genitor. The family takes care of the woman and the children she bore are named after the dead man. Hence, ghost marriage is purely a way of preserving the name of the dead person. It is therefore a social intervention by the living family and clan relatives to marry a wife in the name of the deceased. A close relative is then chosen to beget children. The purpose of a ghost marriage is to avoid discontinuity and to preserve the name of the dead man through the children to be born. In this situation what is important and supreme is the mystical link in the chain of life rather than the biological link.

This type of marriage is common among the *Nuäär*. Ghost is Thuɔm in *Nuäär* language. It is applied to a married person jɔk who was killed. Even if he has several wives, he has to be married a wife from the homicide compensation for his body or lost soul.[15] The married woman would be added to the dead man's other wives as *ciek* tër the wife of the feud. It is important to note that in ghost

---

15   Peter Yiedh Puy interviewed in Khartoum on May 15, 2003.

marriages certain relatives of the deceased could not act as the genitors, because this would be tantamount to incest. Cousins and brothers could marry for one another provided that it is the younger one to do so. For instance, a younger brother could marry for, or inherit the wife of, his dead elder brother but not vice–versa.

4. Child Marriage: Early engagement of spouse

Marriages may be arranged in childhood for boys as well as for girls. Both are pawns in the marriage game. Such arrangements are purely for making alliances where there is an advantage to be gained from that connection. The guardians or parents of the partners are the best judges of the advantages of such arranged marriages. Child marriages are traditionally arranged in cases where an elderly couple bore an only son in their age and probably the youngest. The boy's father chooses a girl for his son, and then proposes to the girl's family. It is difficult for the girl's family to reject. This is done to ensure that before the father died, his son would have children to remember him. The girl is to wait until that boy is mature for marriage. However, this is rare nowadays because of the attendant complications such as reluctance of the girl, conception or elopement etc.

5. Woman-to-Woman Marriage

The *Nuäär* community traditionally practises woman-to-woman marriage, or social marriage between two women. This type of marriage is purely for procreation purposes. The woman who married must herself be a legally married woman who was either barren or had given birth only to daughters. Under such conditions, a woman (supported by her husband and/or brothers) pays bride-wealth for another woman. Just like the marriage of a man and a woman it has the same jural consequences. The wife and children are under the authority of the 'female husband'. The female husband has the right to damages if the wife commits adultery. The children to be produced should belong to the husband's lineage which is the natal lineage of the woman. After initial consultation between herself and her husband, the two choose a girl whom they want to incorporate into their family. The woman, in her husband's presence, designates or mentions the name of the girl to be the wife of her unborn son. The woman's husband then approaches the family of the girl and proposes mare to them. If the proposal were accepted, the girl would be taken home after paying one cow for bride-wealth. The duty of looking for a genitor falls entirely on the woman's husband. The genitor normally is the eldest nephew of the husband. If a nephew was not available, another close male relative is chosen to act as a genitor. There are instances, however, when the woman alone arranged a husband- the genitor. The children born of such union are socially her grandchildren born to her supposed son. In this type of union the genitor is allowed to marry a second wife of his own choice.

Woman-to-woman marriages are traditionally important for the perpetuation of the family's name. The woman who designated a girl to be her son's wife wanted to perpetuate the name of her socially but never biologically born son. Among the *Nuäär*, a barren woman may arrange for a wife in order to provide her with children. She assigns her brother-in-law to fill the male role of negotiating the marriage. The childless woman finds her a husband to have exclusive sexual relationships. The barren woman stays with her wife and the children born to her. But the biological husband has to stay away except that the woman goes to him to get a child. The children produced, however, are considered to be the offspring of the first rather than the second wife.

6. Concubinage

Concubinage is the practice of forming a union with a woman other than the wife. It sometimes refers to the union between two unmarried persons. This may be a commitment with limited rights and duties.

Since no wealth is paid to anybody, this relationship may be regarded as a "poor man's marriage". Even if the man were to support the family, that is not sufficient to justify converting the relationship into a legal marriage. The man cannot demand control or mastery of the home like a married man. The wife's mother and siblings may have more influence on her than him. Concubine is smart in serving the man to attract or ascertain continuity of his assistance and reliance. The concubine may offer her husband domestic services, exclusive sex and support. Nevertheless, she has some degree of independence.

When a couple embarks on concubinage as a union, they must have known each other, had sexual relations and possibly begotten a child or two. Concubinage is not a casual affair to be sealed in a ceremony but it is a serious step. Each partner knows the other can leave the moment he or she is no longer satisfied or thinks can do better elsewhere. But their union becomes stable when they are still satisfied with one another. Where marriage is not possible, a concubine ranks higher than a casual union. *Nuäär* had always recognized concubinage as another way of getting a wife. But this is considered inferior if there is no payment of bride-wealth.

Nuäär take concubinage *luɔm* as a temporary relationship tied with mutual benefits without any marital bond. It is a friendship. The woman friend may be healthy, probably menopausal, and offer good services. Concubinage is not marriage to *Nuäär*. Regardless of how many children he bore with her, the man has no claim. If a man contended with the concubine then died without a formal marriage of *nyadhuɔri*, he will be considered a ghost. Traditionally, his relatives have to marry for him.

7. Levirate Marriage: *kueŋ ciek jɔkä duel*

Nuäär men and women are expected, in their prime years, to reproduce and maintain life. But their sudden death may cause family crises. In that situation, substitute spouses are arranged to assume the roles and responsibilities of the deceased. The most common substitute marriage is the "levirate" that applies to a dead husband. In fact, there is no marriage it is just an arranged inheritance of responsibility to produce on behalf of or for a dead relative. A widow may run away or refuse to be taken over by her husband's designated heir. If she chooses to live with another man, the children they bear are still those of her dead husband. In levirate system, the brother or close male relative of the dead man is made to assume the roles of a husband and father. In such cases, the sexual rights are incidental to the responsibilities of supporting the family and rearing the children.

On the death of a wife, *Nuäär* rarely expect the groom's in-laws to provide him with a substitute unless the deceased had not given birth or given birth to a living small child. The in-laws may offer the groom an unmarried sister of the bride if he were interested to continue their relations. In this case, there are no same procedures of marriage like the original except that the leopard skin chief-Kuärmuɔn, is sent with the new wife to make some sacrifice in that home. His duty is then to separate the dead from the living sister who inherited the home.

The arranged substitute marriage for dead male kin keeps the children for his perpetuation.[16] *Nuäär* society restricts the rights and responsibilities of marriage to the immediate pair. Although they

---

16   Oduyoye Ibid., p. 213.

practice the levirate, they do not allow a man to share his sexual rights to his wife with his brothers. This privilege will extend to the brothers upon his death.

It appears that other levirate practices require or permit a man to marry the wife of his deceased brother. To *Nuäär* this is not marriage per se. *Nuäär* marriage involves discussions and cattle payment culminating into a couple called 'a wife and a husband'. The on-behalf co-habitation is hardly a marriage to the *Nuäär*. The death of the man put off the woman from the house. The dead man's brother has to get her back into the house through an informal occasion.

It is assumed that nobody officially attends to the widow sexually after the death of her husband. Accordingly, if she *lok* rejected a designated person, she would be advised in a family meeting to look for an alternative husband that would 'put her back in the house' and take care of the orphans.[17] She would be a concubine to any person she chose outside the family. Above all a widow would be interested in someone that would cater for her and the children. In normal circumstances, *Nuäär* do not consider going with a widow as an adultery that may incur punishment or divorce. The dead brother is a ghost and his wife should not be divorced on any ground. However, she is respected and consulted on behalf of her dead husband until her elder son is big enough to assume the headship of their house.

To *Nuäär* levirate is *kueŋ ciek jɔkä duel* putting the widow back to the house. It is not a marriage. There are mourning rituals conducted to separate the ghost (dead) from the living. On this occasion the widow is proposed by one person to go with her or she is given alternatives to choose from. If she opted for someone outside the

---

17 The qualities required of him are that he must not have any of the vices *Nuäär* people hate. If he were to be from a background of evil-eyed people, thieves and so on, he would not be accepted to go with the widow. They don't want their offspring to be stamped with such people.

family, she would be advised very strongly not to bring into the family any defects. She becomes a concubine there. But with any of the ghost's relatives, she is not a concubine but returned back to her house with the attendant responsibilities. Although *Nuäär* are not yet proven to have links with the Jews, their levirate motive is in line with what is found in Deuteronomy-the Old Testament, Chapter 25: 5-6. It is clearly indicated that levirate is needed for a legal heir for the deceased so that the dead brother's "name will not be blotted out from Israel". Therefore, levirate is a prime concern among the *Nuäär* too.

8. Other peculiar marriages

Among the *Nuäär* certain marriages have featured their own conditions. These marriages relate to twins *cuë*, monorchids *tor*, left-handed persons *cam, möy,* disabled *kuaruaŋ*, blind *cɔr*, deaf *miŋ* and crippled *duääny*. Next to these is the marriage of a raided person or captive *pëc*. Each marriage is elaborated below.

a. Marriage of twins: Cuë

Nuäär consider twins cuë as one person that just turned out to be two. The first is both (male) or *nya*both (female). The second is bidit/gatdiet (male) or *nya*diet for female. The children born after or following them in sequence are bol, (*nya*abol) tot, (*nya*tot) and *Geŋ* (*nya*Geŋ). The *Nuäär* handle twins in a special way. From early age they move and sleep together until they are ritually separated by their father at the age of twelve years. They can then frequent dances but cannot be embraced nor hands' shaken. They have to be purified *puth* in order to mingle with people. At puberty or adolescence, a male twin shall offer a girl a bracelet and this process is a celebrated occasion with dancing like *buɔr*. If a twin girl had admired a man, she would request to ba ji puth engage him.18 Her father then has to find out if there are relations in case the affair could culminate into marriage. The twins' father offers his daughter a calf to give to the man she chose. A dance occasion has to be organized where the calf daw would be driven to the man's home. In his house, he must slaughter a small bull *ruath* for all those in the dance to feast together throughout the night. During this occasion all those in the dance have to wear feathers of all types because all are assumed to be birds.[18]

When the marriage time comes, there is no other engagement[19] except *cuɛc* betrothal that should take place. Cattle negotiations start normal with the first twin except for the second twin. During the wedding, the husband (or groom) of the twin girl will dress like her and the girl dresses in the civet cat skin. While the *Nyaboth* elder twin's marriage is normally handled, discussed and negotiated the second twin *Nyadiet* is offered or given out for 5-10 cows. Payments and claims of cattle rights are done when their children are married.[20]

b. Marriage of monorchid: Tor

In normal circumstances a *Nuäär* man who started a family with a *kë* and not *nyadhuɔri*, regardless of how many children he had with her, he has to be married a *nyadhuɔri* even as a ghost. The son of such *kɛa* cannot kill any sacrifice for his dead father gat kɛkä me ci guan liu cɛ *yaŋ* näk. But this is opposite to the Tor. It is a *Nuäär* convention that a man with one testicle- monorchid, should not start marriage with a fresh girl. Any monorchid who married a fresh girl would limit her procreation to at most two girls unless a *kɛa* concubine followed in marriage. If a monorchid married a

---

18 Puth is ritualization of a twin to be able to converse and even play with men and girls. It is a step to marriage because it is conducted proce*dura*lly like initial engagement.
19 Abraham Cägh Riäy interviewed in Bentiu on 13th April 2003.
20 This step is skipped as it is assumed to have taken place.

nyadhuɔri, it is catastrophic for him. *Nuäär* believe that one of three things will happen. The first is that one of the couples may die. That failing, their child will die. In the alternative they shall only produce one female child. To avert such a catastrophe is for him to marry a *kë* as his second wife. So, if the tor married a *kë* they will produce normally.

c. Marriage of deficient persons

This applies to a marriage strategy where it is hard for a man to find a wife, and where it is hard for a woman to find a husband. The guardians are concerned to have them married at any price to those who will be useful affines. To *Nuäär* deficiency or disability is not a bar at all. Marriage of the blind, the deaf, or the crippled is different. Blind and cripple ladies are helpless in the house. They are therefore offered to elderly men just to produce children. Something could be got later. There are no discussions, but they are just summoned and informed to have been offered to so.

Regarding the deaf, her father is approached and given 3-5 cows. The five cows belong to the father. The deaf is strong and can work and serve in her home. She is preferably married by an elderly person with children. When the deaf delivers, her entitled relatives demand on individual level. The blind and the crippled deliver under the care of their parents but only go to be impregnated by the men designated. The man provides sorghum and milking cow for the upbringing of the children. When children reach marriage age, he has to settle the bride price so that he can handle the marriages of his daughters. Those entitled are not eager because these are handicapped in any case. Whatever the case, those could not be divorced instead relatives are delighted that the daughter had offspring. If the man rejected her she would not produce but would be married a wife as a ghost by these relatives.

d. The marriage procedures of an adopted person

Nuäär people absorb others into their community in three ways. The first is through raiding, followed by voluntary migrants and the last is through marital relations. An adopted or raided person must first be initiated into spear name of that family. A raided girl, if intended to be a wife, is not caught by the hand. She has to be driven with a shaft. When she is brought home, people have to be invited and a small bull has to be killed as sacrifice to absorb her into the family. If she is intended to be a daughter, then her hand would be got hold of. When she is married, the adopter gets all her cattle rights. If he is to be a son he is equally caught by hand. They are then separated- children from wife. It is a condition that they must not be sister(s) and brother(s). In the marriage of an adopted person, there is no aunt, uncle (maternal or paternal). All the people of rights are not there but they must be considered in entitlements.

If the raided was the mother, she will be absorbed into the rituals and be at home. A raided woman made a wife has to be married. When she produces a boy and he grows big, in his mother's marriage he has to represent the mother and the maternal uncle. He will have the cattle of his mother's marriage. He will pay these cattle during his own marriage as rights which should have been duly offered by those parents. His other brothers will pay towards his marriage representing paternal and maternal uncles.

The marriages stated so far can be severed by relations, incest and other bars. Bars to marriage vary in accordance with social relations. Feud or homicides are some of the remarkable factors that prohibit sexual relations as well as marriage. These are examined forthwith.

II. Sanctioned (barred) marriages among the *Nuäär*

The primary purpose of marriage is the establishing of a family. There are qualities *Nuäär* require of the one who wants to marry. First, the family approaching to marry must have sound background according to the parents of the would- be bride. They should possess the qualities *Nuäär* admire in an in-law such as hard-work, bravery, generosity and oratory. The groom and his relatives should be able to pay the minimum bride-wealth required by the girl's people. The circle of relatives with whom to cultivate relationship should be people of known integrity within the community. Above all the aspiring family should be free from, though minor but are serious, such social issues as theft, asthma, evil eye, etc. These are believed to infect or stamp and consequently bar the next generation from marriage.

In many societies there are rules that prohibit, while others seek to enforce, marriage between persons related in specific ways. A society may be permissive in sexual matters yet limit the category of appropriate sexual and marriage partners. The incest taboo prohibits sexual access to certain categories of kin. The common bars to marriage among the *Nuäär* are:- relationship, sharing of totem, feud or homicide, other minor but manageable issues such as age-set, ŋart (red mouth), thieving etc. Marriage is also prohibited between certain people because of other social implications. It is not appropriate for a *möy, cam, cuääny,* and monorchid to marry among themselves. However, there are bars to marriage which are also reasons for divorce if not realized or ascertained during the initial scrutiny by spouses' families.

Relatives may oppose marriage on the grounds of *liau* (chronic disease) such as *död (*asthma), *dhiil (*leprosy) and *kiɛl (*tuberculosis). A household known for a bad attitude or behaviour or uncordial relations can be avoided in marriage. Family recommendation for the partner to be married is important because the woman belongs to the family and her husband only produces children. The *cieŋ* whole family was involved in the choice and total marriage including cattle payment.

1. Incest taboos

Generally, siblings do not mate, nor parents with children. The breach of this rule is incest. Persons between whom mating is forbidden cannot marry. In *Nuäär* culture, incest taboos extend from members of the nuclear family to include aunts, uncles, and usually first cousins. Marriages between those relatives are abhorred by *Nuäär* society. Incest is abhorred because of the risk of producing severely deformed children. *Nuäär* believe that the offspring of relations suffer birth defects and several of the resulting babies may die. Moreover, to them an incestuous person is vulnerable. He could simply die or be killed by spear, stung by snake, hit by elephant or buffalo, or would fall sick with slimming body. But this does not mean any person that is inflicted in that way may necessarily be an incestuous. Other diseases may have same symptoms.

Incest is sexual intercourse between individuals related in certain prohibited degree of kinship. In every society there are rules prohibiting incestuous unions, both as to sexual intercourse and recognised marriage. Rules of incest taboo prohibit sex and marriage between certain specified relatives. Society condemns incest as a horror and disruptive phenomenon. Incest is an impediment to marriage. The close family members are those related by birth, others related by adoption or marriage. Societies place restrictions on who one may marry.

The *Nuäär* law of incest prohibits sexual play with in-laws, people with blood ties and is also extended to shaking of hands or physical association with specific people. A girl being married to one's cousin should not be caught by hand nor embraced. She is considered wife of a son. There is no incest but a bad habit.

It is believed that if a pregnant woman confessed an incestuous relation earlier, she will deliver with ease. But if she insisted to be shy, it is assumed that she would die at delivery for refusing to confess. Where incest happened long and tiresome restorative measures or cleansing rituals are performed. When incest is confessed, the man who committed it should procure a bull or goat which the leopard skin chief should cut into two. The beast, if a goat, is held by the man and the woman from both hind legs. It is then cut into two with each holding the other leg. Then their mouths are plastered with the bile from the animal. They are thus cleansed.

2. Un-incestuous but selected taboo-associated marriages
(1) *Möy* is somebody conceived while the mother had no monthly period. *Nuäär* fear such an infant because it came abnormally. It is sometimes called strength or outside the compound. It is considered more powerful. (2) *cam* Left-handed is believed by *Nuäär* to be tilted and that means it is abnormal from other humans. (3) Monorchid *tor* and (4) *Dony lεc nhial* first grown-up upper teeth. The first three are abnormal and therefore are avoided during rains.[21]

Mǫy is usually born in front of the compound because it is powerful and therefore catastrophic. It is believed that its mother or one of its grandparents is likely to die. At moon rise the infant *möy* is laid on the road for all those in the home including passers-by to step over it as a blessing. Cooked *dura* is served to the children. The ashes of cow dung are sprinkled into the air and around and then it is returned home. Left- handed, *möy, cuääny,* monorchid and

---

21   They are not allowed to stay indoors with others when it is raining. It is believed that thunder would strike and burn that building because of their presence in it.

grown upper teeth do not stay in one place. They are believed to curse each other because they are powerful. Monorchid and *möy* do not marry left-handed girl and vice versa. Any ram being sacrificed to *möy* is usually hit with a pestle.

3. People sharing a totem do not marry

Some totems start with giving birth. For instance, if a certain child is born deformed and seems to resemble perhaps a *guɔr* (elephant), a *löny* (lion), a *wuud* (ostrich), or *gany* (monster lizard), that particular family will venerate the animal. If someone killed his totem deliberately, it is believed that will cause him to have asthma. Totem is a plant or an animal that some people (families or clan) claim a symbolic association with. It serves as a symbol and focus for that group of people. People of *buoth* the same rights especially those who share scrotum during the sacrificial beast division are members of the same clan. No marriage is allowed between ones who share *juäk* scrotum because they are cousins. So, where relationship is kept there is no marriage.

In scrutinizing marriage, it is necessary for a person to introduce the names of his father, grandfather until the founder of his clan, including their totem, to clarify any relationships involved. This is a guiding chart for the observance of exogamy bars. By knowing their own ascendants, a couple can initially tell whether marriage would be permissible between them. So if they share the same totem that is already their spear name. They should not marry. The totem is a sacred object to the group. It identifies who is and who is not a member of the clan, and whom one may or may not marry. As the lineage and clan trace descent to a common ancestor, they are termed ancestor-focused groups.

4. Relations: *Mar*

Relatives are the people who have descended from one ancestor, acquired marital relations, raided and absorbed into the family, friendship incorporated into rights, one spear-name or totem, age mate etc. These are the relations that are prohibited in marriage selection. Meddling with them would be incestuous, except for friendship which can be broken and converted into marital relations. *Nuäär* are cautious about incest because it is a disease and would also deprive one of bride-wealth entitlements. There is therefore a strong societal control of sexual impulses of the child at an early age. Incest is strongly advised to be avoided by all means. *Nuäär* do not know what to do with a lady one cannot or is prohibited to marry. Sexual intercourse is prohibited as it can lead to conception which eventually becomes blood relationship. The range of close kin prohibited from sexual relations or marriage among the *Nuäär* extends to several cousins, nieces, nephews, aunts etc. Incest is sexual relations between close kin. It is between (a) *nya*muɔlen daughter of aunt (maternal) (b) *nyawacdu-* daughter of aunt (paternal) (c) *nyanääru-*daughter of uncle (maternal) (d) *nyagulen-* daughter of uncle (paternal) (e) *nyimuɔr-*sister (f) *nyanyimuɔr-* daughter of sis-ter (g) *nyadämuɔr-* daughter of brother, (h) *nyagatä wacdu-daughter* of aunt's son (paternal) (i)*nyagatänäru-* daughter of uncle's son (maternal) (j) *nyagatägulen-*daughter of uncle's son (paternal).

The end of *mar* (relations)

Bride-wealth entitlements or rights can severe marriage within the first five or six generations on the female side. But male relationship cannot be erased by rights entitlements. These rights will cease after six generations but that does not justify any marriage though they are more distant kin. The relations or kinship entitlements start with a cow and gradually dwindle to calf, small bull, goat, spear and gourd. This guord is then broken, signalling the end of relations and marriage can ensue. Marriage relationships are terminated, and no other bar can be cited. The end of mar relations is verified by the diagram below. This is the genealogy chart associated with the entitlements of the ancestors which vanish with the guord. In the diagram, Z are the grandparents, A is their daughter while B and C are the sons. As long as the grand parents get rights from the female offspring of A, that are also collected by children of B or C, the relations is still there. Similar rights are got from the daughters of B and C but circulate among them without reaching A. Only one right of the paternal aunt- sister of the father is provided. In this sense A is the aunt of daughters of B and C.

Marital unions between children of brothers, fathers, mothers and other close kin are incestuous among the *Nuäär*. Brothers or cousins of a man are called *cɔw caŋ* (day husbands) of his wife. They cannot go with her for that would amount to incest. The *Nuäär* discourage marriage of cousins. The purpose of marriage is to widen the circle of relatives through in-laws. Marrying non-relatives is to avoid incest where possible, especially in ghost marriage, levirate, and inheritance.

5. Marriage between age-mates and their children is prohibited

Nyariyä du (age-mate's daughter). One cannot nor can one's son marry the daughter of age-mate because she is considered a daughter even, though there may not be blood relations. Age-mates have rights of a *mut* (spear) in the marriage entitlements. There is the age-spear right during marriages of their daughters. *Nuäär* prohibit marriage of age-mates unless one of them had died between the two families. A bull calf is driven into the *luak* below the *gɛn*[22] and tied

---

22   The sleeping stair erected above the fireplace inside the *luak* is called *gɛn*.

in the *luak* as *cut* (compensation) to the dead age-mate. But if it is a ghost marriage for elder by a younger generation- this law does not apply when both age-mates (father of the girl also and the ghost) are dead. Similarly, any cow slaughtered for a dead age-mate is not eaten by the surviving mates including the other meals. Feasts and celebrations or all the festivities are attended but not enjoyed by the surviving age-mates. No surviving mate would be offered something in the utensils used on such occasion. These things are prohibited, and it is believed that any age-mate who tampered with them would be contaminated. To rectify it the dead age-mate is to be compensated with a spear, or ram or small bull with which to throw away a tobacco by elders saying that *kuiyɛ ne ji* 'forgive him he is ignorant about you'.

a. When to and not to marry *nyaricädu* age-mate's daughter

In case a son wanted to marry the daughter of his father's dead age-mate, the surviving mate has to provide a small bull *ruath* as a reward for the dead one. This *ruath*, is not just driven, it has to be ritualised. All the surviving age-mates have to pray to their dead colleague that "let the people be related don't be angry with us son of our mother, take this cow". It is then taken home to the *luak* and dragged under the *gɛn* and throughout the *luak* and is then tied down on the poles to the right of the byre. The man whose father has been compensated is free to do anything with it. This cow is not refundable even during divorce.

b. Dropping out from an age-set to another

If an age-mate wants to marry from daughters of his age-mate, or their children to marry themselves, he will decide to drop out from that age and move up or down. He will provide a *ruath* or ram and call his new age-mates. They pray over it and the master of ceremonies is

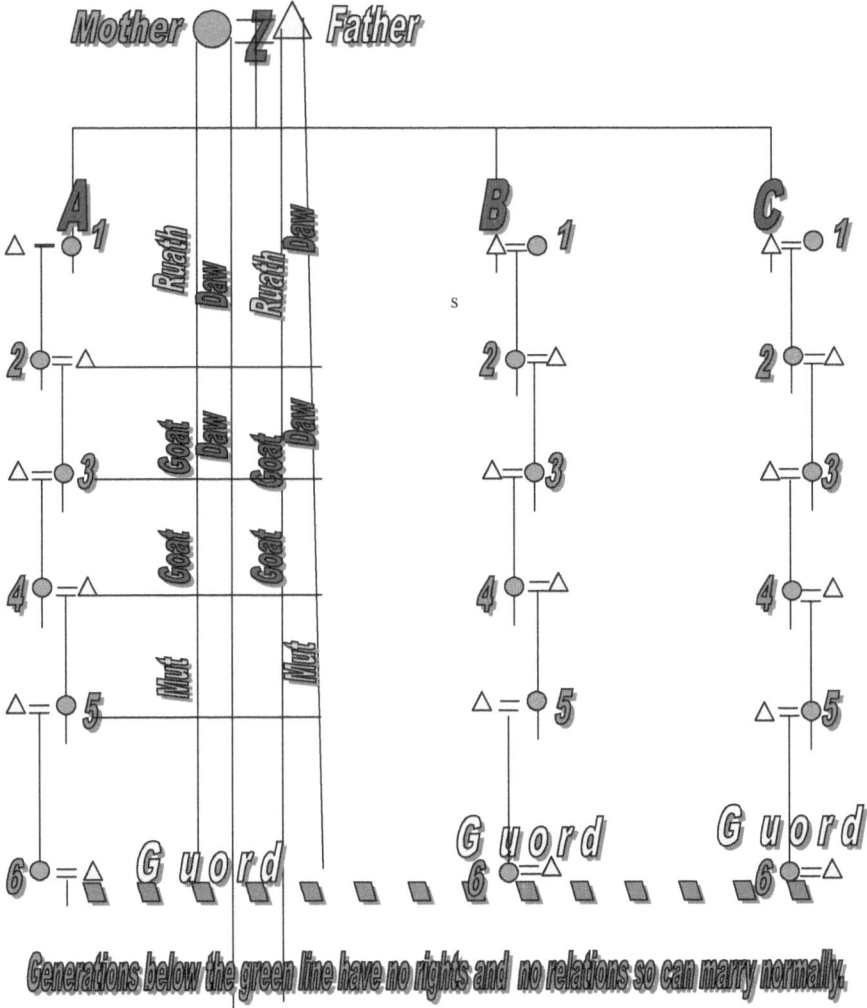

Source: Author's own drawing

summoned to kill it. He is then separated from that age and attached to another one. *Nuäär* call it 'the separation of generation' *däägh riyä*. Those who initiate the marriage are the ones to drop out.

Dropping out of an age-mate to give room for such marriage is to skip the bar provided. Some were married to or by upper or lower age-set to his present one. Otherwise, it becomes troublesome if earlier marriages took place with one of the generations he dropped to. This would affect all his children most rather than himself.

A man may be attracted by a girl and propose to marry her. But if the girl informed him that her father was his age-mate, this man will give the girl a bracelet from his hand.[23] He then orders her to inform her parents that an age-mate of her father offered to marry her and so had given her the bracelet. She should say this upon her arrival at home. The essence of this *ciɛy* (bracelet) is the admiration the man had for her. During her marriage this man (girl's father age-mate) shall be given a *ruath* small bull with which to return the bracelet to him.

6. Other social factors for family integrity

There are issues that can discredit a family because of background of one member. The family is very careful about that. These are some of the factors considered during the scrutiny of the spouse by their respective families. Those that can discourage marriage because of bad image likely to affect the family are considered serious in marriage. Apart from (a) divorce that can sever remarriage, the ensuing issues can severe/sanction marriage or incur divorce when discovered or committed during the marital life. They are:

(b) adultery, (c) attempted suicide, (d) gossiping, (e) thievery, (f) evil-eye, and (g) red mouth.

---

23   According to Mahmoud Ruɔt Kaŋ (died) a *Nuäär* Muslim who grew up in *Nuäär* land before he embraced Islam.

a. Divorce: Dägh

If a woman urinated on bed by mistake, the husband sends her away and she proceeds to paternal uncle who must pay a cow as *cut* (compensation). If she repeated, she would be divorced straight away. Similarly, a woman who is dirty, clumsy and unable to care for the man would be divorced. These same reasons are social bars to marriage. Any families known to have such shortcomings would be avoided in marriage. In normal circumstances, a woman cannot be divorced in a year of acute hunger. Even if she committed a mistake, she should not be divorced because it will be an insult to the man. People will say he divorced his wife because of hunger. The divorced woman shall be described as the one that was divorced from so - a divorcee.

However, divorce is not an easy process because it is affected by the repayment of bride-wealth. In this case, the woman's kin usually tries to patch up the differences and consider the rights and wrongs on either side. But ironically, the son-in-law to *Nuäär* is always right. When it is the woman divorcing, unless she convinces her parents that the gravity of her husband's offence outweighs the socio-economic advantages of their relations, the bride-wealth beneficiaries are always reluctant to accept. In extreme circumstances, she might by-pass her relatives and go to court. If the court accepts her case, she would be charged to collect the wealth from her relatives and handover to the husband.

She failed in most cases and only run away from the man but remains a roaming wife of that household. Any children she begot with anybody should *duly* belong to the bride-wealth owner. In a normal divorce, the man can remarry on his own behalf no family contribution since he was emancipated from his father's authority during the first marriage. He has greater freedom of making spouse choice. The divorced woman cannot be remarried but taken by another man as a concubine with no bride-wealth. But if she was officially divorced with original bride-wealth totally reclaimed, she can be married as a second wife with little wealth- six cows only.

b. Adultery: Dhom

The beauty and power of attraction of a woman induce men, other than her husband, to desire her. When this woman goes with another man then adultery is committed. If a woman committed adultery, it may be solved by force (fighting) or peacefully by the neighbours or people at home. Whether this is a cause for divorce or not is the decision of her husband. But for the widow, it is not the case. She continues with full marital rights to be the property of the spirit of her deceased husband.

If a woman committed adultery, her husband has to be compensated by the adulterer which the cousins of the husband will collect there and then. If the husband feels very bitter, divorce will follow normally. It is no more the issue of dishonesty by the wife but the *kɔɔr* side effect of adultery. *Nuäär* believe that *kɔɔr* is like incest in the body. The body turns grey with a noticeable slimming and shivering. Kɔɔr is a disease one contacts when his wife had committed adultery on his bed with another man. To cleanse it the man's master of ceremonies has to be summoned to sacrifice a cow in front of a hut. The hut is purposely made of grass to be set on fire with the husband and wife inside. They are to rush out of the burning grass hut. Kɔɔr is believed to have been left burning with the hut. It is a part of contamination that should be redressed by earth (leopard skin) chief or man of spirits. The wife taken by another man is a shame no one would swallow. It would indicate that the woman had a low opinion or disregard for the man.

c. Attempted suicide: Daph

If a woman tried to commit suicide or poison herself, this is an indication that she does not like the family and would therefore be divorced. Such families do not attract others in marriage.

d. Gossip: Löm

A woman gossiper can cause conflict within the community and bring troubles to her home. She would be divorced. Offspring of such families are usually avoided for fear of injecting such personalities into the family. Family of the would-be-bride can reject marriage to a man from family of such background because they would be bad in-laws.

e. Thievery: Kual

A woman who stole something, maize or *dura*, from the neighbours or anywhere, how trivial that may be, can be divorced. The fear is that the bad name will be associated with or stamp the children. *Nuäär* nickname a thief as somebody with a nail. The objects are stolen with the tip of the nail without being noticed. So a thief is assumed to have a long nail with which to pick things. Families known for thievery are hardly attractive to be in-laws. If married by mistake, they are divorced unless there is evidence that stealing was abandoned.

f. Evil-eye: *Pëth/Pɛdh*

An evil-eyed family are the usual suspects of the ills in the community. They are associated and targeted for any illness that occurred to a family whose house they passed by or entered. They face beating and isolation in most cases. Similarly, no people want to relate to them and inherit evil-eye through marriage. So evil-eye *pɛath* is a social bar to marriage. However, *Nuäär* believe that an evil-eye act can be redressed or neutralized by another evil-eye.

g. Red mouth: ŋart

A bar to marriage against a man is *ŋart* (red mouth). It is a reddish spot in the mouth just the upper or lower part of the lip. This is believed to kill the woman. So, a man having this would not be accepted to marry. *Lokɛ rami thök ŋart.*

7. Feud/Homicide

Whenever death occurred between families because one of them killed a person, their relations are no longer cordial. They are in a feud bent on the intention of revenge. But if the homicide was handled through cattle compensation, each relative would get his/her entitlement. This is the same entitlement in marriage. With death between them, no one would accept both entitlements from one person for the two incidents. *Nuäär* contamination would occur which is catastrophic for the entire family. Therefore, feud is a bar to a cordial relationship. Hence marriage is prohibited. Homicide can result from fighting with spears, stick fight, killing or death by mistake etc. In all cases of homicide, there must be death and cattle payment. Any child born to the aggrieved family is then named *Ter*, *Thoŋ*, *Taŋ*, *Mut* etc. Children are thus named to continue the feud and remind them later. There are songs by children that say, *ɣac, ɣac, ɛ dhol e näk guadɔŋ ɣään!* "Oh dear this is the boy who killed my great grandfather". This is a reminder to the children that there is feud/enmity existing between their family and that of the other. Even with the settlement of a feud, they still can't eat together because they are enemies for life though hostilities are suspended. They cannot marry nor eat together. In communal gatherings (cultivation or other occasions) they don't sit neither over one table nor drink or eat from the same utensils. They have to be separated. It is the death that accounts for the bar except in certain situations considered below.

A person killed through a duel of stick fight is also homicide. Somebody killed unintentionally is settled through payment of 30 cows only. No imprisonment because it is an accident. Though an accident, it is a bar and has to be managed through a ritual- a bone is to be broken.

An eloped girl who died in the hands of the eloper is compensated with 30 cows. This is considered a mistake not an accident. *Nuäär* call it *Thoŋ yikä* 'mat homicide' which means that she died on a mat.

Guääc (cɔay). Accident (killing) leading to death is a total bar to marriage because the taboos associated with it will make life difficult. *Te kamdan kɛ cɔay* 'We have a bone between us' means that a standing physical person has been knocked down or broken by one of the families. This falling of a person due to killing becomes a feud that even compensation cannot erase. Compensation can, at most, reduce tension and sever relations. The grieved people cannot enter into marriage relations with a culprit. These families are enemies though have been quietened to end the feud. This deadly act between them cannot make any marriage cordial. It will be found that they have a feud. That is a sufficient and serious bar

Marriage between feuding groups is also a taboo. In sentiment *tɛr* (feud) is forever. The spirit of vengeance is there and, should an opportunity avail itself, that family would be targeted most as the real enemies. In practice, *tɛr* (feud) is a bar to a relationship forever. A *tɛr* (feud) that took place five or more generations before on the female side can be broken to enable marriage to take place. On the side of males it is to continue for life. When a quarrel ensues with in-laws and death occurs, the daughter/wife of the slain family will be cut-off to her husband's side. This is done to avoid *nuer* (contamination) and ensure that the children to be born do not enter the feud. This daughter has thus belonged to her relatives by marriage.

8. Homicides not bars to marriage

There are other homicide cases that *Nuäär* do not consider serious enough to bar marriage. They were committed as accidents. Moreover, some of them are from relatives who cannot be in feud. These exceptional homicides are accidents, not mistakes.[24]

a. A husband killed by his wife

A woman who has killed a person is homicide. The woman who killed her husband has to be helped by the husband's step-brothers to pay blood wealth to the child of the husband's other wife (co-wife). Not a single cow should be brought from any of her relatives. If the woman has children they have to divide themselves. Some will stay with the mother until the kuärmuɔn settled the matter.

b. Baby killed by sitter

Bed homicide is when a baby-sitter killed a suckling or weaning baby by accident. The baby/infant could have fallen or just die during warm water bathing. The baby-sitter could be a sister yet the blood compensation must be done to avoid *Nuäär* contamination. It would be handled as an accident. Six cows are paid in compensation- the sixth being a ram.

c. A pregnant woman raped and miscarriages

A pregnant wife, if raped by another man and the child is squeezed out - this is considered ɛ *Thoŋ yikä* homicide on a bed or a mat. Such a child is compensated with 3 cows and a ram is there for sacrifice. This *Thoŋ* yikä has no cow to kill for rituals. It is just settled by *kuär-muɔn* the leopard skin chief, not in costume, as a mistake. Should a *kuärmuɔn* be the offender, the person doing the ritual has to put on civet cat skin, not leopard skin.

---

24   Guäc accident is unintended but duɛr mistake is consequence of an act.

d. Accidents

Somebody can be speared during fishing and die. This act is accidental. This could be compensated but cannot bar marriage. The leopard skin chief *Kuärmuɔn* will handle this mistake without a leopard skin and pray to God that, "It is a mistake". He will address the dead person that, "Turn your head, you are not killed intentionally it is an accident don't be angry let it just end here". The *Kuärmuɔn* can break the bone of a ram. He will make each of the families catch it on one side and then he breaks it. Or he can chop a straw into six pieces and distribute the six of them and the families break them.

CHAPTER TWO
The Evolution of *Nuäär* Family

Introduction

The act, formality, or ceremony by which the marriage union is created differs among peoples. An earlier entry custom into the marriage was the capture of the woman by her intended husband. At face value, this act could be regarded as a means of getting a wife, rather than the formation of the marriage union itself. But the symbolic seizure of wives continued. It has become simulated and looked upon as the whole marriage ceremony or an essential accomplishment of it. Various other ceremonial forms have accompanied or constituted the entrance upon the marriage relation, the most common of which was some kind of feast. It is a custom among the *Nuäär* that marriage has to take place in a formal ceremony.

It is worthy to note that the couple have decided to undergo an irreversible change of status from unmarried to married. Hence this marriage represents their attainment of full adult status and the beginning of a socially recognised domestic unit. To found a *Nuäär* family there are generally three steps to follow- courtship, betrothal and marriage ceremony. In pre-arranged marriages like that of the child, woman-to-woman and ghost, courtship would be missing with betrothal only formalized before the marriage ceremony. However, there are other minor steps wedged in-between them to make a total of thirteen steps until the consummation of the marriage- making the *Nuäär* family. The marriage ceremonies are rites with features. The first action is engagement *luɔm* which means that the man and the woman had promised marriage to each other. This is a betrothal- the initial part of the deal. It is remarkably a formal way of giving notice that a particular man has reserved a girl. The second is the wedding *buɔr*, where the bride would formally be given to the bridegroom by her father or guardian. The father or guardian would speak to the groom that, "Son of …I give you my daughter". In the *Nuäär* context, this is usually done in a bride's home. The third is *muɔt nyal* or bedding in another context. In some societies, the couple were expected to go or actually went to bed together in the presence of witnesses. To *Nuäär* this live-show of sexual action is never called for. In *muɔt* where the bride is formally introduced to and welcomed by the family spirits, it is implicitly established that how soon a couple would go to bed together is nobody's concern.. People raise concerns when pregnancy does not show at a later stage.

A wedding actually affirms, before the public, what the two couples had privately committed themselves to. Through the wedding, the couples are connected with friends and the community who acknowledge and witness the event.

The above stages are preceded by a transitional process that follows a chronological sequence right from childhood to full maturity with an independent home and children.

I. The Transition Stage

Transition involves both male and female except that the latter has few indications. First, she is a *pith nyal*. *Pith nyal* is a girl approaching adulthood- she is not yet a woman. Her breasts just appeared. When her monthly flow (menstruation) has come, the women say that *buɔdhdɛ payɛ wäy* her hunger just disappeared or finished. A girl that has menstruated is usually designated a milking cow by her father to feed on. She or a woman in the house will milk it. No butter should be made from the milk of this cow because no other person is entitled to use this oil. When she gets married she leaves this cow at home. However, she may be given the calf to take to her new home. But the cow and its remaining offspring have to be cleansed so that the men at home can then drink its milk. First, the tail of the mother cow is cut a bit and then it is driven to the river. Cleansing of mother cow should equally be applied to even its off-spring.[25] If this is not performed, *Nuäär* believe that the cow and its offspring will be contaminated.

Shortly after puberty, *Nuäär* young men undergo an initiation involving scarification. They are thus initiated into adulthood which admits them into a system of social hierarchy. In this hierarchy, each person is provided with knowledge of his status in society. One is made aware of his link with the past as well as the future responsibilities corresponding to the level he occupies. The reverence for the immediate older generation and the younger generations is an obligation. They thereafter become warriors for a period of 5-7 years, after which they are allowed to marry and have children. They become tribal elders.

The emphasis is the transition of a male child moving from the house where he was born to the *luak* byre. Within the *luak* he passes stages until he marries and moves out to establish, in turn,

---

25 Thomas Tot Baŋɔaŋ interviewed on August 16, 2003 in Khartoum.

his own *luak*. This is the transition from childhood to adulthood and marriage before death.

A baby boy and a girl grow in the hut. The growing male child parts with the mother in the house at the age of eight years. At puberty age, the boy goes to the *luak* byre to sleep there and the girl remains in the *duel* house with the mother. The girl undertakes some care and is actually assigned domestic work by the women. She cleans the compound of cow dung, grinds food, goes to fetch water and firewood, drives the calves to graze and back in the late evening and ties them down. The boy herds the goats and calves. He tethers them too. He progresses from tending goats and calves to caring, tethering, and herding the cattle around 12-15 years old. During the rainy season, in the morning, he ploughs with the big people. He is consequently approaching the age of scarification by the new standard. Previously, he is half mature man. When he is 15 years or about that, he will be marked mostly in November-December. He spends one and one-half months confined in the house until the scars are fully cured. Their group is graduated by January.

a. Scarification (marking): *gäri*

The initiative for marking usually originates from the father. He may feel that his son is mature to endure the incision and so informs him to be ready for marking towards the end of the year. It is an important stage that entails preparation and sacrifice. Some food deserves to be pre-positioned for the occasion and the two or three months feeding of this boy. To the father, the scarification is a project and an important event to the entire family. The boy is eventually heading towards forming or making his own family. The occasion is a transition for the woman (mother of the boy) in the household. From that day onwards she is promoted and recognized as a cousin and would not be divorced under any circumstances. She can misbehave within limits and would not be admonished like a young lady. Moreover, she will behave respectfully and responsibly towards the people. She can be a mother -in-law through her son.

Sometimes the boy reminds his father about his intention to be marked. In fact, his age-mates in the village confer to be initiated and inform their parents accordingly. If the father does not approve of the request, he will discourage the boy at that time. The father disapproves of *gäri* if there is no *dura* hence no food to feed on for three months or there is a major construction activity of a byre that is taking attention. If the father hesitated to permit him, the boy may just join his age-mates in the marking against the wishes of his father. When he has persevered the *gar*, his father then becomes happy with his vigilance. If the boy's age-mates are due to be marked gared, (this is the word gar only borrowed to make pass tense) he may join them in disregard of the fathers disapproval. He will be described to have cɛ rɔdɛ kual *gäri*- stealthily gone to be marked.

The scarification is marked with serious dancing, drinking of beer and eating of meat for two to four days. All the fathers, mothers and paternal uncles of the boys to be marked are to conduct this dance. No youth are ever invited to attend the *bul chɔati*- dance of the hairless/hornless scarified boys. This is the ample time both parents had waited to air out their respective grudges against each other. They had composed them in songs that are recited/learned there and sung in common by all of them. There is neither bitterness nor fighting. The *puoc* (shyness or shame) is to cease henceforth and both behave like cousins. During this period these parents jump, dance and run around chasing and beating themselves at random. Some mothers' *yaat* (skirts) are forcefully plugged off. It is an insult for her to be stripped naked and laughed at by cɔu caŋ her brothers-in-law.

So, at this stage, the mother has become a man wut in the house and is therefore *cɛ la gatgulen* (like a cousin). But if the dance *bul chɔati*, for any reason, could not be conducted prior to *gäri*, it must be made on the day of their discharge with sacrifices made – one day feasting only.

After the elders have cleared the beer, food, meat, the jokes and sung songs against themselves, the children to be marked would be assembled in one big *luak* where they would be marked. *Gäri* is usually in mass. A group of 4-10 boys are marked together and have to feed and sleep in one place as well as walk together until they are discharged after six to eight weeks.

The boys are shaved with a piece of hair left in the middle of the head for the master of ceremonies to plug and throw away during his prayers for the boy. They are assembled and a bull is offered by one father. This must necessarily be the father of the eldest or first son to be marked in that family. This animal is to be sacrificed. An elderly man of the village, preferably one *rui* with some communal authority and respect would be informed to (invoke) *lam* on the occasion. The prayer is to God, "for the newly scared to have the wounds fast healing, protect them from harm and misfortunes, let peace and health be upon us all here. Any ailment one has should be carried by this animal". *Lamkɛ je ɛ dit i "a garkien kot, kä a puanykɔ puɔl. Mi tɛkɛ rami te kɛ lɔɔb, ba baph ɛn yaŋe bä` näɣɛ"*. A few others may pray or just rub the animal's back with ashes. Tobacco, water and ashes are applied. The master of ceremonies will have to peg down the animal. The eldest person spears it. Its carcass has no entitlements but just randomly apportioned to those who attended the occasion. The person who scarified the boys is usually supplied from the sacrificial meat, offered his own quantity of beer and a ram by any of the boys' parents.

The boys lie down in a row within the house compound and are marked in turn. Each boy is laid on a hole into which the blood would pour during the marking. The first mark on the forehead is called *wöi dhɔl* 'relegation of boyhood'. The fathers and mothers are present witnessing the action. As soon as a boy is finished and has endured to the end his mother would yell. So, the occasion is full of yelling and much talking encouraging the youth to persevere. The ones who stopped bleeding would be rushed to the house designated for them. That house is purified, clean and free of mosquitoes. All this group sleep in this same house. They move for courting girls *luɔm nyiet* when the scars have healed. It seems a convention that a marked youth should not go to the cattle camp that season. He has to be nursed because he lost much blood *kɛ yo ci riɛmdɛ lony.*

Gäri scarification or initiation was started long ago. Its purpose was first for *Nuäär* to identify themselves and the *gaar* (marks) became six. These six incisions are put across the forehead within the range of three inches from above the ears upwards to the centre of the head. One boy may get seven marks through a technical mistake from the *gäär* (marker). Mistake as it is, that boy later enjoys priority, if not seniority over his peers. In the distribution of meat he gets the lion share and before his peers. The second reason was for division or categorization of age (segmentation) so that respect and difference are there in sitting or even in the division of food.[26] Finally, gääri bars or restricts one from certain activities. For instance, when one is 'gared' he cannot eat *tɛaŋ*[27] and should as well abandon the milking of cows. The house of the mother and father should not be frequented or entered. Should he wish to fetch

---

26   Michael Tɔi Jɔak (late), 63 years old. Interviewed on March 25, 2003 in Bentiu.
27   There is a small gourd or mud plate on which food is put for the small child to eat first to quinch its appetite. This *tɛaŋ* is that food offered to make the child avoid the temptation of snatching food and perhaps linger around and fall into hot food with serious burn.

something inside he must order or call for it from outside. Any of his spears or sticks must be hung outside the house. If there is no body to call and fetch the thing in the house, then one can enter, pick what he needs and come out without sitting.

"*Gäri*" seems the most emotional and important moment in the life of these youth. It is full of restrictions that actually reflect the change in behaviour and conduct of the young man. The new human being is contained to attitudes supposedly relevant to his new status. Marked boys do not go into the *luak* because they may step on the cow dung that is assumed would blur their scars. A newly marked fellow is like a *pai daph* recently delivered woman who does not enter the cattle compound. It is only when the child's umbilical cord has fallen that she passes through to fetch something in the *luak*. Similarly, a newly scarified person doesn't pass among the cattle or herd unless the wounds (scars) have fully recovered. That is when they are about to be discharged after 28-30 days indoors. If this is violated, they are likely to contact *thiaŋ* and it is believed that their marks begin to cause pain. A man who goes with his wife cannot contact the *chɔat*.[28] They have to be cleansed by letting them step on fire to protect them from *thiaŋ* unless they have wristlet skins of tiang. Of course, the *chɔt* period is partially a fattening project.

They are not greeted by handshake lest the scars inflame and bleed or they contaminate. They move in the farm but not in the compound, not to step on cow dung. The cow dung is believed to have *thër* a disease that would inflame the marks. They come out and enter into the house from an outside gate. Just like a gate cut for the groom to enter the bride's house. Respect starts from puberty. At this age or stage he is advised against talking anyhow because he is now a man.

---

28 *Chɔt* means hornless or naked head. In this context the newly scared youth are described by their hairless bald heads *chɔat*

b. The conduct/behaviour of a marked person[29]

A marked man does not milk a cow. If certain circumstances forced him to do so, he must not drink that milk. It has to be drunk by others who are not his age-mates. That cow has to be cleansed by cutting its tail with the ceremonial spear. Grass and water would be poured into a fresh gourd and the cow is then driven to the river, beaten with the grass soaked in water from the fresh gourd. The cow must cross to the other side of the river or stream with the people. If this is not done the cow will *Nuäär* contaminate.

Courting starts during the period of nursing (from scarification) when the group marked together move out as from 4 p.m. chasing any girl and asking her to *luɔm*[30] chose any of them. What is required of her is just to select by pointing at or show of hand. The girl will select and point at one young man. There is no mention of name but only counting of the girls one has so far-fetched. It becomes apparent that the one who has more is the likely one to have more lovers in future. Young men even joke with each other that "I surpassed you since that time of scarification and still continue to date". The final count is that so and so has 30-50/60 girls who chose him. It is not anything but selecting or choosing one from the group who could possibly have been a friend.

When the *chɔat* should be discharged is decided by the father of the one in whose house all those *chɔat* were "gared". He will invite the fathers of all those marked together that "the children have to be discharged". He provides and kills a bull. This bull is to be sacrificed for them all but one of the fathers will do the prayers. The one designated to do so will plead to God that "These who have been marked, let them breathe and also let peace and good health prevail in us". There is a bul dance by elders where

---

29   Thomas Tot Baŋɔaŋ, interviewed on August 6, 2003 in Khartoum.
30   *Luɔm* in this context is choosing of *chɔat* and no more.

they are free to insult themselves in songs but without bitterness. Every disgruntled man or woman always wished for this occasion when all the odds could be done with impunity. No punishment, no quarrels but drinking and singing and playing throughout the night. There is plenty of beer to drink and food to eat.

The *chɔat* are stoned with dry cow dung and driven to the river in the early morning. This is a sort of blessing. They bathe and come out. Needless to say, they haven't been bathing completely but partially without watering the head. The grass ornaments are removed or cut off. The young men are sprayed with ashes of cow dung and then let to enter into the byre. The 'gared' boy is consequently graduated, becomes a man to stay in the *luak* with elders and go to dances with them. Upon his discharge he goes to the dances. Sometimes he may go to the cattle camp where a friend may introduce him into manhood- the way he should behave or talk to girls and others. If he is so weak in courting girls, in dances, he will depend on friends of his elders for almost two years. Alternatively, he may not go to the camp but stay at home with the mother that season. He gets nursed and made ready for rainy season dances.

When they are discharged, each young man goes to a paternal aunt, having the same spear-name, to be given a bracelet. Then he proceeds to his paternal uncle to offer him a spear. He goes to the next uncle to give him a spear with or without a stick. He keeps collecting from relatives until he has fetched six pieces. Those who were marked during those five years are a generation.

Around June- August of that year, the young man courts girls, runs to dances, and is able to compose songs because manhood has appeared in him. He is to run after girls, sleep away without being questioned. Soon after this he abandons tethering cattle, he is not a boy any longer but a man. He will be given spears, do some hoeing[31] and drive cattle to the camps with his sister(s). In case there is no younger brother, the father may request to borrow son of a friend, sister or relative to look after the cattle and he grows up in that family.

This stage is the formation of songs and conversation with small girls of 9-12 years old. From this group the songs he composed, and his voice are heard generally. The big girls may be attracted to him to listen and recite his songs at times, and eventually end up as his lovers for the coming few years.

If he is the elder son, the girls may admire him for marriage. But if his elder brother exists and not married, he then just enjoys conversation with or courting girls without marriage. He is, however, expected to show much respect and establish good relations with all the elders, age-mates and, above all, with girls. When his elder brother marries, he is then pushed up in the marriage priority list. During the third year, he can fight people with spears but not stick fight. He fights with sticks only with age-mates but not the elderly. But if an elder person aggressed him that should be handled by that man's age-mate among his people. The elder son who married must be made an abode to settle on his own within two years.

The above transitional stage must be followed by the formation of a family through the procedures henceforth. The *Nuäär* marriage process involves sixteen steps. These are (a) kääm *tuac*, (b) selection and scrutiny of spouses (both bride and groom families), with consensus of spouse choice, (c) the groom declares his marriage intention *läär nyal kuen*, (d) the girl takes the intention home to her parents *läär cieŋ* where the *kuud* is screened, (e) the groom is accepted and love communicated back to him *läär nhok*, (f) *kuud* declares booking the girl- *luɔm nyal*, the initial and formal marriage

---

31   The *Nuäär* saying 'duth bul kä liɛc kay'- 'dance but don't neglect the field'

commitment, (g) *paph yiɣni (määtni tuaini)*- In-laws Joint Council Meeting is scheduled, (h) the young man decides to (betrothe) *cuicäkä* the girl, (i) marriage or bride-wealth negotiations *tuɔc* are determined, (j) *buɔr* wedding ceremony follows, (k) the girls have to strip the *kuud* of the civet cat skin *luony tuaini* so that he does not go to the market in search for a wife. (l) The groom arranges to *muɔt nyal* take the bride. He must meet or talk to the mothers-in-law *ruac kɛ manthuɣni* before doing so. After the mothers time, the other elders give them advices on how to handle themselves at home and generally with the community. (m) The wife is taken she has to be dressed- *ruɣ yɔaɣ-yaat.* (n) The bride is at home the husband must step on the feet of the woman *dɔnyni cioy ciek* i.e. take their private time at home. (o) The next is womanhood *mään-ba nyal wicdɛ luɔc jɔk.* (p) The early action is for her to cook- *that.* Each step has a special meaning and significance in and of itself. Some of them have ceremonies and rituals, others are just necessary steps. They are all linked and follow the same sequence. Each step is detailed below. It starts with the offering of '*tuac*' civet cat skin. This is permission to marry which is usually given by the father or paternal uncle. There is much rationale in giving it. It could be given normally or on condition. This shall be verified forthwith.

II. *Nuäär* marriage preliminaries

Nuäär marriage is making of a family that is conducted on two levels. Level one is the guided choice of a partner *nyadhuɔri*. An unmarried fresh girl whose choice follows *Nuäär* conventional steps is called *Nyadhuɔri.*[32] The most popular form of marriage seems to be the *nyadhuɔri* system that facilitates the voluntary union of the male and the female. This is the ideal marriage that is

---

32 Dhuɔr are tassels that are worn by girls. These dhuɔr are identified withfield'   an unmarried girl. So a fresh girl is *nyadhuɔri.*

handled in the coming part of this work. This type of marriage is applied as conventional because it starts with (1) *käm tuac* licensing/authorization from the parents to a *kuud* with associated behaviour. This is followed by:- (2) choice and screening of a spouse, (3) *Läär kuen* - (declaration of marriage), (4) *Läär cieŋ* - (home report) (5) *Läär nhok* - (declaration of acceptance), (6) *Luɔm* - booking (7) *Paph yiɣni/määtni tuaini* - In-laws Joint Council meeting, (8) *cuɛc* - betrothal, (9) *Tuɔc*-bridewealth negotiations, (10) *Buɔr* - wedding, (11) Luɔny *tuai*ni - untying the civet cat skins, (12) *muɔt nyal* - taking the wife. (13) Ruɣ yɔa - dressing the woman and (14) *Dɔnyni jioɣni ciek* - stepping on the woman's feet. (15) The womanhood stage- *mään ba nyal wicdɛ luɔc jɔk* is a formality. This is followed by (16) *that* (cooking) - that is the last step. It is necessary to note at the outset that the elders are fully involved in numbers 1, 2, (advise on 3 and 6) 7, 9, 12, 15 and 16.

The second level is the marriage of the *kë*. *Kë* is a second-hand girl. A girl eloped or impregnated and abandoned is considered *kë*. In rare circumstances she is re-married as *nyadhuɔri* with all the procedures initiated. She must have been ritually married before, perhaps gave birth once and then divorced for a reason. She could be re-married without undergoing those steps again. A few cattle-probably twelve to fifteen heads of cattle, are paid for her marriage. When these have been paid, she goes to her husband's home accompanied by a small girl. This is sometimes considered the marriage of a poor man who by-passes the steps. *Nuäär* usually wonder, for an unmarried person, and ask if he is so poor as not to afford a *kë*. So *kë* is the cheapest to acquire in marriage. She is, above all considered carefree. *Nuäär* say that she was the first person to break certain illusions held in regards to the earth. It was said that the *Nuäär* people of long ago used to walk very slowly and carefully on the earth for fear that it might be punched. *Kë* saw the cow of her child suckling. Fearing that all the milk would be depleted by the calf, she ran to save some milk for her child. She did not bother if the land or earth collapsed and so broke the myth.

Therefore, the *Nuäär* considered that the *Kë* had created problems for them. That she tampered with the earth pushed the sky farther up and severed direct links with the *ran* (human being). They composed a song that described her identity. It states that a *kë* walks carelessly, conceited and carefree, and with a hanging frock. She has nowhere except to migrate to the Dinka land where she might be married in the diaspora.

Whether the marriage is of *Nyadhuɔri* or *kë*, there are two types of marriage. These are the 'arranged marriage' and the so-called 'love marriage'. Arranged marriage is when young people have no free say regarding the choice of marriage partners. Young people are helped in choosing their partners. There are situations when the young man chooses but is scrutinized by the relatives. At times the parents made the choice and proceeded to arrange the marriage based on friendship[33] and other qualities of the girl and her parents.

Accordingly, normal *Nuäär* marriages are arranged with a guided choice of a spouse because of *tuac* giving and the concept *"ciek ɛ ciek cieŋ"*. The two levels of responsibility that predominate *Nuäär* marriage are the spouse choice and bride-wealth payment. In arranged marriages, the whole responsibility of conducting and consummating it is collective. The collectivity of *Nuäär* marriage is reflected right from the courtship. Because parental consent is required in the marriage arrangements young men are regulated in going around the procedures. But in the marriage of second and other successive wives, these are out of love under the responsibility of the man alone. It is more appropriate for the initial marriage to be arranged than to be out of love. However, love marriages do take place.

---

33   Breaking of friendship to give way to marital relations.

The second is the 'free choice' or marriage of romantic love. A love marriage is where the couple agrees to marry without the assistance of a go-between or matchmaker. The relatives may, or may not, be involved in the last stages. This type of marriage, though familiar, is self-imposed on *Nuäär*. In certain circumstances, *Nuäär* condone individual partners' choice or love choice. One circumstance is marriage to a non-*Nuäär* lady without scrutiny or procedures. Nothing demands the participation of the groom's parents because there is no cattle payment requested by those entitled from the bride's side. This is a personal effort marriage and relatives are only informed.[34] Another marriage is through conception as a result of a love relationship not necessarily targeting marriage. Through love, the man may entice the girl into sexual intercourse. Sometimes they discuss before action. In case the affair resulted in a conception and the man reneged, she has to summon him before his relatives or brothers to inform him that she will not give up the one who impregnated her nor abandon her child. This talk may grade her a reasonable lady worth marrying. The family of the man will force him to marry her. Such a marriage has no regret from the couple for they loved each other.

A groom must have engaged the bride in the process. Somewhere in the mid-way of formalizing the marriage process, the groom impatiently undercuts those procedures by eloping the girl *kuel nyal*. In *Nuäär* marriage, this is one way of circumventing parental choice and forcing the consent of the elders to a marriage. Though the man was officially accepted to marry and undertook some procedures, he might fear that another fellow would run away with her and so why not him. When they decide to elope, people remark that the groom has run away with his wife. There is no bitterness. The procedures are then completed by the elders.

There is another elopement *tɛkɛ kuel* by force. The lady is forced

---

34   John Wicjial Kueth interviewed on 17th September 2003 in Khartoum.

or rather raped and blackmailed into marriage. Captured and raped, she would decide to go with the person who abused her virginity. Otherwise, she can refuse him and opt to be second hand- *kεa*. Such a marriage would have problems if she was engaged and betrothed to another person. This can cause fighting. Despite all this, the bride's people can decide to return her to the previous applicant or groom if he was still interested in her. But should he give up, the second man would be forced into marriage without the blessing of the relatives. Such marriage is usually considered inferior because *muɔt* and *buɔr* were not conducted. Many cattle are demanded and collected by force from the new groom because of his misconduct *dhɔal* in the whole affair. This marriage has come by capture, not a choice. However, this way of circumventing parental choice and forcing the consent of elders is not a good/blessed marriage.

A young man of marriage age, able to handle household responsibilities and has cattle with which to marry, would be asked by the family head to find and bring any girl that attracted him for marriage. If the procedures were acceptable to both families (of the boy and the girl) then arrangements would be made for them to marry to form their own home or household. The relevant conventions are followed to conduct the marriage. This is the ideal marriage of *nyadhuɔri* which we shall describe in detail later.

A young man and a maiden who loved each other and accepted to be bride and groom have to get married. But a boy of age who died of sickness or mysteriously is a ghost. He has to be married a wife to form his household. The children begotten on his behalf are called after him.

But before the man and girl marry, certain precepts must take place. The girl and the man meet in a dance, on the road or anywhere. They start teasing each other leading to a mutual conversation.

Initially, the man would request to know the name of the girl. It should be noted that age-sets dance together. Related young men of the same village make one dancing (fleet) *dep*. They should know any girlfriend or acquaintance of either of them. Should any fleet member meet a girl separately, he will first inquire whether the girl knew any of his fellows and he starts naming them. If the girl knew none, this gentleman will display himself alone, a solemn request to be acquainted. The girl may accept him. In this case he will jump up, *muac* and sing a short verse from one of his best songs. He will declare his name and bull name. The girl then will respond similarly. They depart on the understanding that they shall meet another time. But if the girl rejected them she should wish to be excused as she was in a hurry. The man, without bitterness, shall know that they have been rejected and so the girl is let to go in peace.

a. Käm Tuac: civet cat skin giving either normally or on condition. Once given he becomes a kuud whose behavior should be pleasing.

Boys usually marry above the age of twenty- four and girls between fourteen and twenty-two years. The first step in marriage is an understanding reached between a father and son that the son will marry, the initiative originating with the father or uncle. The father voluntarily gives him the *tuac* civet cat skin without the boy requesting it. The paternal uncle also offers the *tuac*. He may offer it during a dance when girls encircle his cousin.[35]

After courting girls for five years, the father may wish that the boy marries a wife for himself. Sometimes if the boy overstayed without being licensed or authorised, his uncle (paternal) may ask the brother- father of the boy, why so is not marrying. Authority to marry is offered by the father on the son's behaviour and availability of bride-wealth. Maybe the son has bad conduct and needs time to

---

35   Malek Duph interviewed in Bentiu on April 16, 2003.

adjust. If the father likes his son he can be delayed up to seven years. Or if the son does bad things his father may decide to rush the marriage in case this responsibility may reform him or make him adjust from his behaviour. On the other hand, his father may probably observe, or be made aware of, how his son is courting and dancing with many girls.

The father may sense that the son will be trapped into impregnation of a girl or two thus disposing of cattle through *ruɔɔk* (compensation) of tort. He will tell the son that "these properties may disappear and moreover your mother is ageing and the responsibility and work are heavy on her, better find a wife, a good girl (If the father has not one in mind)". The father gives him a *ruath* (small bull) or *dɛl* (goat) to buy the *tuac* (civet cat skin). The boy owns this *tuac* and runs to all the dance occasions with it. The initial contact and meeting places for the young people are markets, cattle camps, schools and churches for Christians but not at their homes under any circumstances. The other occasions are dances and marriage ceremonies. The *Nuäär* commonly know that whoever wears the *tuac* is looking for a wife. The girls are keener about that. It was indicated earlier that an untargeted girl could impose herself by grabbing the *kuud*'s bulls and wish that she could thus be married.

As noted earlier, the young man dancing with the *tuac* throughout is looking or actually preparing to choose a wife among all the girls. His age-mates become aware too that he has been licensed or authorised by his father to marry or look for a partner. The *tuac* giving, with a recommendation or direct choice, is a provocative act for the fathers of this boy's age-mates. Therefore, a sequence of *tuai* giving follows. A licensed young man must be given ivory armlets and a civet cat skin to wear so that he is accordingly recognized.

Nuäär believe that *tuac* must not stay long because a catastrophic situation may happen that would do away with all the cattle. Should there be adverse reports about the son, his marriage will be hurried hoping that he would adjust as he gets responsible. A man admired or loved by girls may be contempt and beaten *thum baŋ* by some envious persons. He may beat others in turn. In any fight if the fingers are broken, the thumb and the last finger are compensated. Those are some of the factors to speed up the marriage once initiated.

The decision to marry involves no discussion but information from one source of authority-the father. The father of the household who decides such matters is the custodian of family wealth-cattle. He is, as well, the keeper of family welfare and therefore keen about marriage priority list within the family and the clan too. So when the father proposes the marriage, he has already designated certain cattle towards the marriage and continues to collect more. The youth offered the *tuac* is already mature and there are two cows. *Nuäär* would hardly announce the total of his cattle. He lumps them as two cows or one calf.

The father normally gives his son permission to marry without conditions except the reservations listed above. He just summons and informs the son that "I feel that you can construct your own abode". There is no response from the son. Prior to that he may tell his wife that, "the son is now entitled to a wife, what do you say?" In case she has objection on her son, she may instead tell the husband to, "Marry another wife, at least to relieve me from the burden and the co-wife would help in the upbringing of the children. Your son can marry then."[36] She should be interested in the administration of the home. This must be a monogamous family with sufficient cattle wealth for both marriages. If the man insisted to let his son

---

36   This is according to David Duɔb Puɔc of Akobo interviewed on August 15, 2003 in Khartoum. The other versions of Nasir and Fan-gak (Gawäär) are condensed on pages 80-90.

marry, he will not take her proposal. In the next few days he will call his entire family to inform them that he has authorised their brother to look for a wife. This is just giving of information without discussion. He does not want to surprise them when their brother gets entangled in marriage.

The young man having been offered a *tuac*, his father will inform him that, "I belong to such a generation (age-mate), you must not marry from there". He will continue to show his son the front (elders to the father) and behind (the younger ones). The father continues that, "Any girl related to us do not invite for marriage this is *gɔl* because you share spear name. Avoid families having a feud with us".

A youth offered *tuac* during the rainy season would wait until people move the cattle to the camps. If he targeted to marry a certain girl in that camp, he will run around the camp with his bulls. The girl may take the whole of the bulls and tie them down in her camp. The young man returns to his camp singing. If another, untargeted, girl got hold of them, these bulls have to be returned even by force if she dared not to release them. Force is likely to be used to have them released and returned. Sometimes he will tell the girl that, "I was emotional. I was not offered a *tuac*, leave the cattle". She may release them but the issue goes around that the bulls of this young man, were caught by the daughter of so. The boy's father may hear about this at home. Depending on whether the father has sufficient favourable knowledge about that family, he will seldom interfere.

Behaviour of a kuud

With this approval, the young man has become a *kuud*. *Kuud* is a young person authorized to marry. He is pushing to another status. The person undertaking the passage from one status to another must abandon certain attachments and habits. The *kuud* must learn that, in the life cycle of individuals, role changes do occur in a regular and predictable way. The role changes maintain some connection with the physiological maturation of an individual. The individual enters into a new relationship with the world and the community. This relationship subjects him to new opportunities, new dangers, and new responsibilities.

A young man authorised to marry undertakes decent behaviour. His life must change and be commensurable with the married life. He is then expected to prepare to be self-reliant, independent and responsible. Once married, he has entered into a circle of extended relationships (in-laws) and formed a new era of solidified friendships through cattle payments in the bride-wealth.

The licensed young man does not chew cane, beat a child nor stone a dog. He does not walk anyhow but dresses smartly. In behaviour, he should be respectful to all the age-mates of his father-in-law and those related to him. Disrespect would offend and strain relations. A story to emphasise this is often related about a maternal uncle and his sister's son. The cousin was marrying the daughter of an age-mate of his uncle. The boy was reported to have uttered an insult to his uncle that, "These remains of chewed *dura* cane must necessarily belong to *liɛr* age-set". *Liɛr* was an age-set to which both the boy's maternal uncle and his very father-in-law belonged. During the marriage of this cousin, his uncle paid his six cattle, but at the end declared the marriage dissolved because of what his sister's son had uttered earlier on about his age-set. He had to be cut compensated. An offence to an age-mate is marked and must be redressed as it can strain relations. A milking cow was paid in compensation and offered to the bride's father. So, one has to tie his tongue if not married.

Families spend a great deal of effort and wealth on the make-up for the groom and the bride, as *kuɔɔd*[37] people licensed for marriage. Decorated dresses, at least two ivory armlets, beads, necklaces, earrings, and a variety of human adornments are availed. Thus, in addition to protection, modesty, and adornment, the dresses serve a number of less obvious functions. In fact, they make the properties or the dowry the bride carries to her new home. She would be stripped of the maiden ornaments and given new ones by the groom's sisters. Therefore, if she goes without, the groom is usually paid a cow *yaŋ guɔri* in lieu.

The *kuud* must exhibit good conduct. He should not stone a dog because that is a sign of dar (greed). He loves children, is calm, polite, gentle, enduring, self-restrained etc. When he goes fishing and spears a fish, he does not stoop to fetch fish because that will dirty his ring, ivory and expose his underpart to be looked at. He walks sideways and leaves the road to the approaching elders. When people cut grass over a beer or food he must not appear there. If seen he would seem to have gone to look for food or beer.

b. Selection and scrutiny of a spouse

The selection of a spouse for the son of the family is a collective responsibility. There should be an exploration for a beautiful girl who stayed too long without being married.[38] It will be ascertained whether she had any contact, adverse or otherwise, with a cattle chief, *kuäär yɔɔk*. *Kuäär yɔɔk* the cattle chief could curse a girl also or anoint a girl and get a *ruath* small bull during her marriage. Any person who anointed or quarrelled with her is to be asked because both are either a blessing or a curse. This is important to note in case she is admired by the *kuud*.

---

37   This is the plural of *kuud*
38   Small children are the real source from whom to extract such information.

However, the marrying young man initiates the choice and subjects her to scrutiny by the entire family. Since the *Nuäär* guiding principle in marriage is that the wife belongs to the family, all have to participate in choosing her. She will accordingly be incorporated into that family or clan. The young man is at times helped, by the other relatives, of who to approach for marriage. This is based on the personal knowledge of each relative of the families with girls and of sound background. Each family has its own conditions of the type of girl they would wish to marry and by extension have relations with her parents. In the end, the family consensus after serious scrutiny, would be considered the household choice.

To the *Nuäär*, a woman's value is only in her capacity to bear children. Infertility constitutes the main reason for which a man can change his wife. In some aspects of *Nuäär* ceremonial life, fertility assumes special importance in the choice of a wife. But men also search for qualities of kindness, congeniality and a stable marriage partner who will not run away with other men. In addition to the girl's state of health, her ability to look after calves and till the land are important considerations too.

The *kuud* courts the girls and starts pinpointing some. Regardless of whether the *kuud* boy has a specific girl in mind, the father may direct him in the meantime to a selected girl from a family he (the father) admires and wishes to have relations with. If the son agrees with his father's suggestion, he usually calls on the girl himself to ask her if she wishes to marry him. The young man will then get to know the girl through his sisters and other brothers or cousins. It is quite exceptional for a boy to develop marital understanding with a girl without having first discussed the question with his father.

The most common departure from the ideal just described is for a boy to disagree with his father's choice. It then depends on the father's authority whether his will prevail. If the boy refuses the girl chosen for him, his father usually asks him whom he wants. Personal relations within the elementary family will determine the result, in each case. A father may direct his son to particular families that are admirable, decent, rich, and of the qualities. Despite the fact that the father has the decisive word, he does not enforce all or the majority of the marriages. The son has a good opportunity to express his own opinion and can win his way in many cases.

A father's choice may not be to the taste of the son *kuud*. The son has to convince him to give her up. The father may ask about another family that has a daughter with a good lifestyle. But any family that is pieγ of low productivity would be abandoned for one with kuai seeds or offspring- high productivity. When the groom has brought a girl that is acceptable to his parents and relatives, he will be instructed to, "announce marriage to the girl".

It is probable that the young man may be attracted to and initiate conversation with a girl he found in one of the places he frequented. With their relations progressing cordially, they may agree to marry and push their issue formally to their respective parents. Accordingly, the *kuud* informs his father and they make a general review of the girl's family- their feminine origin, attitude and excellence. They also explore relations or other bars to marriage. The virtues of hard work and cleanliness are scrutinized right from the mother of the girl in case she is like or resembles her mother. When it is ascertained through the scrutiny that there is no relationship or other strong bar to marriage, the young man would be advised to declare to the girl his intention to marry her.

If the *kuud* got attracted during the year his female relatives- sister, niece, nephew, have a secret deal or understanding with him to commonly scrutinise any lady brought. So, whenever he saw a girl, these relatives will furnish him about that girl. If they do not approve of her, she will be abandoned until an acceptable one is found. He also informs his mother, wife of the brother, and his married sister(s). The scrutiny had thus passed from the girls to the women in the family. These women go around asking the women folks (age-mates) they used to dance together long ago. They continue the search, for almost two months, to be able to know more about the girl.

The women are concerned with her family and the girl in particular. They wish to know: does she wash dishes? Cares for and likes the children? Tethers the cattle? Likes elder brothers and sisters? How about her cleanliness, economy in food storage, procuring of firewood? Is she a good and fast cook, hospitable and receptive, polite, hardworking? Does she milk without depriving calves of milk? Does she clean the *luak* of cow dung or leave it soaked with cattle urine causing mosquitoes? Does she pour all the milk into the gourd without any little to remain with children? When cooking, does she taste the food or give children first and follow later? Are the utensils prepared before or after cooking? Is her porridge not clean? Does she grind fine or rough powder? Is her milking gourd smelling? Is supper at sunset or late in the night? How about breakfast- early or mid-day? Does she care for the small children at home, especially their feeding? How does she look at her mother's co-wife?

At supper time, are their spoons noisy? During early rains, does she store firewood or only snatches grass and cook with it? Does she protect the plants and/or seeds from domestic animals? Is she jolly with guests? Does she serve guests with food or water? Is she rude and aggressive when talking or she is normal between the family members or even the guests? Are the house and the compound in front plastered annually? Does she taste the food while cooking it? Is she known for fencing their home after rains? Does she take permission to go for a dance or not? How soon does she return from dancing places? These women highlight the good virtues, attractive to them, to warrant choosing her for a family wife.

Consensus on spouse choice
Those who participate in the choice of a spouse have kinship ties. They participate effectively as well as indicate the rights and duties of the individual parties. The usual persons involved are the potential spouses, their fathers, their uncles, their mothers and possibly their brothers and sisters. The bearers of ultimate authority are the two fathers. The explicit right of a boy's father to choose the bride is based on his kinship position and on his duty to pay the bride-wealth. In the choice of a marriage partner, the son's duty to obey his father is reciprocal to his right to have the bride-wealth paid by his father. However, the son has the informal possibility of trying to persuade his father to agree to his own choice. A girl has no such opportunity; she must obey her father's decision unconditionally. Therefore, a *Nuäär* girl cannot force unwilling parents to agree to her marriage with a lover. This happens to a married woman who left her husband to live with another man of her choice that cannot or will not pay any bride-wealth. Her case then concerns the actual husband and the new lover.

c. Läär kuen: Declaration of marriage
Marriage intention can be relayed through the girl, a relative of the man, the bride's father, or the groom's father may select a home or clan he is interested to have relations with. Any relatives of the girl and/ or the boy can propose marriage. Other sources, apart from the girl, have to be scrutinized by the family council (father, brothers, and uncles- maternal, of the girl). They review the origin and the decent families (of sound standing). One of their consensus may have more cattle. The parents of the girl may be approached for

marriage of their daughter. Her parents would summon and inform her that, "The family of so intend to marry and came through us what is your reaction?" If she has respect for her parents she will yield to their choice. Otherwise, she is at liberty to reject or go against her parents happen what may. A dilemma ensues when two or three applicants are all acceptable. They may vary in the total cattle each possessed. The first come is handled first and the rest are advised to wait until this is finalised. He will be told *tucni* to proceed with cattle counting while the other two who also have supporters from the bride's people are equally working to undermine this in favour of their own choice. Whoever will have more cattle is the one to be asked to marry. If there are many suiters she may tip her parents that she used to be intercepted by people who may intend to elope with her. This however applies to a girl with no brothers to protect her.

The relatives will then report to the man that "she is a nice girl except we are not certain if she will accept you in marriage or not". After this women's report and his lengthy discussion with the father, the young man *kuud* then approaches the girl. He will call her by night at the dance that "Dear lady, I want to marry you for a wife, what do you say?" The girl may answer " I shall think over it[39] and inform you in 7-10 days' time". From now onwards the *kuud* goes by day time around the home of the girl he has in mind. He converses with her outside the homestead of the girl but a visible place from the house. He would be offered tobacco to smoke. This mission would be repeated three times. During the third time, he will introduce the topic to the girls "You have seen me come time and again because I have something in heart". The girl then request that, "Can you tell us what it is?" The *kuud* answers that "I came purposely to meet and tell you my intension to marry a wife".

---

39   Not an immediate positive or negative response. She gives herself and relatives time to study and scrutinize the man.

The girls would advise him to "Be specific". The specified girl may say "I have not yet thought about it". The *kuud* departs to return after a day or two for confirmation so that he finds an alternative soon if rejected. After the *kuud*'s departure, the girls confer among themselves for a response, favorable or otherwise. He returns for the fourth time to inform the girls that, "I came for that talk. What have you thought about it?" If the girl rejected him he will be told plainly that "it would not be possible, you are rejected". But once he is told that "You have been accepted", he will reply that "I shall come after (this number of) days with another man". The *kuud* chose to handle the matter himself in order not to be embarrassed by refusal before many young men.

Since he has an initial approval and acceptance, he can confidently bring other fellows to this company of girls. The *kuud* goes to his friend (best man) to inform him that, "I have found a girl whom I want us to see and contact". They come and sit in that same spot the *kuud* used. This time there are more girls and men. The plan is that the *kuud*, with his companions, would introduce the marriage intention anew. The best man will announce to the girls that "We are having a marriage plan". The girls will ask again, "Which girl among us?". Once the *kuud* has given the name the girls then pull away to confer. They come back to declare that, "Your talk was listened to and you are accepted". The companions of the groom would say, "Declare us in the *luak Läär cieŋ*". Accordingly, he has declared himself for marriage. But the girl's consent is contingent on the approval of her parents. She should then take his marriage intention/message to her parents. Upon this information, the girl's family also do receive and scrutinize the applicant(s) that aspire for marriage.

d. Läär cieŋ and scrutiny of the kuud

However, *läär cieŋ* has some problems when marriage is declared by a person not favourable to the girl. Sometimes a mature girl who does not like a man for other reason(s) but does not want to be blamed by her parents for rejecting a man there and then[40] would report him at home. The man may have a lot of cattle and so her parents would be angry with her for such an absolute action. In that case, she will have to announce or report the man's intention to her parents. Her parents may accept the man to marry. Despite all this arrangement she is bound to inform the man that she doesn't love him. Probably she may have been attracted by another young man with good songs. But the man will insist to pursue the marriage despite her disapproval. Under such circumstances, the girl's parents may invite the candidate for marriage discussions.[41] The father of the girl will force her to accept the process. He will summon his daughter that "I heard that the son of Mr… has expressed interest to marry and you turned him down. I want that family so I can benefit from them. Therefore, tell Mr… to let his son, who expressed interest to marry my daughter, come".[42] After this information, both fathers would arrange to start talking over the issue. This marriage is usually rushed by skipping engagement and proceeding to *buɔr* to discuss the marriage details. Because *luɔm* and *cuɛc* are disregarded or undercut, the marriage is termed '*kuen kol*'. This is to say that the marriage or wedding was discussed over the *kol* sitting skin straight in disregard of other steps. Only the big people started everything from the discussion table neglecting the youth's role in it.

---

40 A girl has not absolute right to reject applicants there and then.
41 Bride's father's initiative in response to his daughter's rejection without reference to the home.
42 Diu Kuɔk interviewed in Khartoum on August 17, 2002.

(i) More suiters to marry[43]

Marriage could be introduced through the girl's relatives or parents. Sometimes two or three fellows or applicants may meet over one girl for marriage. At this stage, the girl may be suspended temporarily from attending dances until the family has conferred over this issue. Normally, the father is supposed to call his wife and then the son(s) to inform them that, "our daughter will, from today, not attend to any dances until I inform you". He will then summon all his cousins to inform them about the prospective husband from among the candidates. Serious scrutiny takes place household by household and individual by individual. Whoever they have agreed upon, the father communicates to the wife, son(s), and the daughter. He will strongly advise the daughter that, "the son of Mr. so and so... has been accepted, and should come forward for discussion". The girl will inform the chosen fellow to present himself procedurally. Henceforth the marriage moves from individual initiative to family collective responsibility.

(ii) The girl's family receives and screens the applicant

But referring to the case of the *kuud* procedurally handled above, the girl accepted the marriage declaration and reported it home for further scrutiny and remarks or confirmation. While the girl conveyed to her parents that gentleman's marriage intention, she has to learn about this fellow from her brothers who frequent dances with him. It may be that her brothers would tell her that socially he is not a good man. But if the brothers' report is positive for the man, the girl has to confer with her mother, over the man, whose consent is prime.[44] Her mother will also search about the boy's mother and

---

43　　Related by Peter *Taŋ* Dundëŋ who was interviewed in Khartoum on June 10, 2002.
44　　This is informal. The father is the one to inform the whole household after his consent.

sisters. She may find them probably evil-eyed, thieves, robbers, troublesome, gossipers, or hungry people who are lazy to work (not hard-working). They may be poor people without cattle and do not farm a lot.

But if the mother favoured him, she would advise her daughter to proceed to the father. At a convenient time and place, morning or late evening in the *luak* or the house compound, the girl would sit near her father. This is not an ordinary act but an indication that she was approaching him on an important issue for discussion or information. Her father would listen to her story about marriage intention by a certain man. The father would ascertain her love for and acceptance of that man. She may say that what matters is her father's general approval. The father should accordingly inform his daughter on his positive or negative background about this man's family. If for any reason(s) he would not opt for relations with this family, he has to convey to his daughter why those people do not deserve to have relations with them. The father's unilateral rejection might convince his daughter to abandon the programme. She should then inform her lover that things are difficult at home. If they are in deep love they may defy their parents by eloping themselves. But if things went well, the father would tell his daughter to invite the boy for discussion of other steps towards the goal.

Alternatively, upon the first information, the girl gives to the father, he may instruct her to inform her paternal uncle; maternal uncle or an intimate friend of his. She will report back after having relayed the information to those assigned to her by the father. After all those steps the bride's father will summon his brother, friend and brother-in-law for consultation on the information that "son of so is reported to express interest in our daughter. What do we know about the family of the boy?"

The girl's relatives then confer on their own and look for (1) possible relations on father and mother sides, (2) homicide and (3) move to inquiries on the family- the boy, father and mother, regarding *riob* thievery, *waŋ* evil-eye, mistakes and accidents deserving chut compensation. The respective preliminary investigations show nothing discreditable in the ancestry of the prospective partners. Therefore, the girl's father's final report may be that the character of the prospective marriage partner and the circumstances of his family indicate that there is "no relations or homicide between us".[45] Any other minor issues may be raised during the marriage discussions. The father then asks his daughter, "Do you accept them or how is it?" If she answers positively, he may direct her to "Let them come". The bride's father may consult or just inform his son on the matter. Otherwise, he would give direct approval to his daughter to inform the boy to report his case. The girl's father has granted his consent to the marriage. The girl's mother cannot oppose nor forbid the marriage because her husband has expressed his and consequently their consent.[46] Nevertheless her attitude is usually known. But if the marriage cannot take place for obvious reasons, then the aspiring young man is informed, through the girl, to abandon the idea or plan. He has to comply. But if he is in deep love with the girl he may force his way through and so decide to elope with her. Such a situation normally creates a fight between families because the act is considered an intended disappointment.

The *kuud* was reported home where he was thoroughly scrutinised. He passed the test and was finally accepted for marriage. The girls are then instructed to convey-*Läär nhok*, accordingly.

---

45 This is an invitation to come forward with the proposal.
46 Among the *Nuäär*, the mother has more influence on her daughter. So if she opposed such marriage her daughter would hardly forward the matter to the father. Connival of a mother and her daughter over a gentleman of their liking but rejected '*luak*' normally leads to eloping and/ conception.

e. Läär nhok- confession or return of love i.e Marriage is acceptable to the big people at home

Normally the home report could be accepted or rejected. In both cases, the family opinion or consent must be duly relayed to the aspiring young man. The information is fed back in two ways. The negative one (rejection) is discreet while acceptance is made a big occasion by the youth. In the negative sense the girl may report that, "Our talk will not be possible it is unbecoming, nothing was accepted about it". She must state if the rejection was from the youth or others. The brother of the girl may pretend to object as a threat in order to be pleased and be offered a good bull. But if her parents were the ones who objected then she will confess that, "The people of the household rejected it". An indication that it was the girl's parents who rejected relations with the man's parents. During this occasion, there is no singing they just disperse without bitterness. It is usually from 3-5 p.m.

But acceptance can be singly or collectively handled as detailed below. Carrying a positive report, the girl may go with her companion and inform the man in their usual meeting place-probably the dancing place, the good news of his acceptance at her home. Upon this information, the young man takes another step to engage her on a day he fixed for the girl to provide feedback to her parents.

A second method is that the girl invites a few girls in her village to a nearby home, designated and prepared for the occasion. In front of the *luak* is an open space where the gentleman intending to marry would be summoned, with a few of his walking mates. It is usually about 2 p.m. There is no single refreshment apart from the shade. That day becomes an important occasion for all the youth. This occasion is well marked by the youth because they confer alone without any influence from elders although it is remotely monitored. They run around jumping in front of the designated byre. In that place, the girls make confessions of love. The girls sit on one side and the boys sit facing them. The girl proposed for marriage is placed or seated in the middle of the girls. Similarly, the wedding boy is seated in the centre of youth. The youth have a leader, mostly their orator, to open the talk. He may start with a conversation and face a girl of similar quality or status on the girl's side. They gradually enter into the issue of marriage from among the girls. When the young men utter 'marriage', the girls' leader will ask, even if she may know him, "Who is marrying among you?" The youth may dodge for some time but eventually confess the name and point at him physically for the girls to see. After this introduction, the youth may request the girl to stand for all to see her. Perhaps the youth may want or prefer to see her nude and so order her cloth to be removed. The girls and the youth will all look at her. The would-be-husband is also asked to stand up to be looked at. When they are ordered to sit by either of the orators, they then start talking.

The boys explain to the girls the reason for their coming that "We came to ascertain your acceptance for us". The girls' spokesperson may answer that, "We have accepted you". One of the men may wish that all the girls say so or the girl wanted should confess alone. Depending on whether the girl is shy or not, she may or may not express it. During this discussion, all the youth from both sexes had talked. This confession or declaration of love for one another is a prerequisite for marriage. The information extends to all the people through the youth that marriage intention has been announced with love expressed between daughter and son of such families. The youth had expressed their love and to be followed by the elder's role. The young men would then say "As you have accepted us, we shall engage the girl". *Luɔm nyal*.

At the end of this confession, *läär nhok* the would-be-bride in-forms her sweetheart that she would come to his home on such a day to return her love for him. On that designated day she would take along a good heifer to the groom's place. The offering of the heifer to the groom is an expression of her acceptance and love for him. Her friends, younger brothers, and other youth from their village accompany her. They arrive at the groom's place at 2-3 p.m. where they are well received. The groom and best friend pull aside and start jumping, running around in happiness and singing. All the youth companions join them and the occasion breaks into singing.

The girls tie the heifer they brought in the groom's compound and leave it behind. Meanwhile, they are shown seven to ten cows that may include one milking cow, selected for them to take home. But if they were not satisfied with that, they would be reluctant to take them. Instead, they may opt to select the cows acceptable to them. They would take these cows and tie them down in their own *luak* byre without an occasion. These cows are neither for booking *luɔm* nor *cuɛc* engagement, they are *lɔl* cows given out of pride to show off about the marriage. However, these will be allocated during the marriage betting stage- *tuɔc* the bride-wealth negotiations.

f. *Luɔm nyal*

Both methods are followed by *luɔm* booking-the second to the last step *cuɛc* by the youth. From these occasions, the affair has to shift to the fathers and senior relatives of the young people. This is further handled or detailed in the consummation of marriage item I (a) in chapter three below.

Another version by-passes the return of love (*läär nhok*) and goes straight to engagement *luɔm*. Once a girl has declared acceptance for marriage, the young man (son) accordingly informs his father that they have been accepted to formally come forward. His father will order him to *luɔm* engage her. The young man decides to engage her and summons his fellows for the occasion. The information is duly sent to the bride about the day of engagement or booking. The youth and young wives of the groom's brothers or cousins assemble to take five to ten cows to the bride's people as engagement. They should arrive at the bride's place around 2-3 p.m. With that number of cattle, in the bride's compound, the young man has engaged *luɔm*. *Luɔm* is a formal declaration and introduction to marry. This is the wedding youth's second to the last step after their respective relatives have given provisional consent for the marriage.

Henceforth, the other steps of *tuɔc*, *buɔr* and *muɔt* follow to consummate the marriage. The groom's father formally asks for convening of the marriage. Through those processes, the people enter into rituals, festivals and ceremonies associated with marriage consummation.

III. Rituals, festivals and ceremonies

Among the *Nuäär* people, birth, naming, initiation into adulthood, marriage and funerals are peak moments in their lives that are ritualised. The community participates in these "... traditional rituals which mark stages in the life, passing from one stage to another through a sacred event".[47]

This stage involves the rituals, ceremonies and festivals that are incorporated into some of the ensuing steps connected with the marriage. Large numbers of people are gathered and given feasts for their entertainment. The two sides of the kin have an obligation to meet this expense. These actions are crowned by blessing lam of some form. The prayers and invocations with the instruments and articles used deserve a mention for a better follow up in the course of the marriage.

The *Nuäär* community has developed their own typical

---

47   Parrinder, Geoffrey, African Traditional Religion, 3rd ed. London and New York:Harper and Row, 1976 p.79

ceremonies. Many of the important incidents in *Nuäär* life survive and continue to be celebrated because they are prescribed and approved by their culture including those they adopted and developed. So, their ritual culture is still extant, preserved, and practised by them even now. The rituals become a meaningful part of the communal life of the *Nuäär* people by sharing in common whatever is around those rituals.

The rituals of engagement and marriage ceremonies are conducted in many ways. The *Nuäär* words for the process of booking an engagement between a couple are *luɔm* and *cuɛc*. These practices are on set dates usually negotiated and agreed upon before the wedding. They consist of a feast laid on for many guests.

Nuäär weddings are organized huge events full of excitement. The wedding is a deliberate, ritualised, recurrent action, complete with gesture and nuance and part of a good form of life. When family and friends join the couple in this celebration, this reflects their commitment to the marriage. It may have gathered people scattered across long distances. Such festivals are the occasions that gather people across long distances to eat good food and drink fine beer. The meal together becomes a reunion with old friends and the making of some new ones. In the community life is centred, ordered and sustained through eating, drinking and feasting together. The participants, therefore, enjoy all manner of relaxation.

The master of ceremonies of each household is very instrumental in the carrying out of the matrimonial duties. To him, it is a routine which involves directing how the seating, negotiations, prayers and other ceremonies should proceed during the marriage. The master of ceremonies is there from both sides of the marriage parties.

A *Nuäär* marriage is incomplete without a blessing of some type. All prayers in *Nuäär* ceremonies start by asking God to bless the couple and make the ceremony run well, to ward off any evil eyes that may come upon the happy occasion. This festive occasion is usually held in the late afternoon.

When a *Nuäär* calls upon lam God in ritual, for instance, he calls, 'WAH! Guandɔŋ'- meaning 'Oh! God of the great-grand father' he means exactly the one in their myths whom they believe is associated with this ritual. God may be called by different names and personalities. They may also call on other spirits of a separate and equal entity. These are usually the family traditional spirits residing in the other world- jɔɔk, or jɔgi- behind there. Most *Nuäär* see this as the unseen part of their world. The jɔɔk are believed to have power, rights and obligations towards those living. Thus, the spirits who are contacted during ritual are already there. So, interaction between this world and that other world is constant with and without the ritual.

Lam could be (1) for removal of mourning. In the first instance, the people praying have to inform the son about the death of his father and that he must know the extent of his responsibility to the household henceforth. (2) an initial sacrifice upon death, (3) protection or cure from ailments (disease, death etc), and (4) blessing for marriage, initiation (scarification).

In lam there is a serious plea to the divine will for protection and the physical wellbeing of the people. In so doing, the *Nuäär* man believes, and is completely certain, that the answers to all the problems of the universe, including his own, are in the hands of the divine authority.

The person prays saying, "The moving wind, if you so will (wish), such and such should happen". This is an earnest appeal to God. If it is good or bad, it is believed God will reveal it in few days. *Nuäär* believe that human being is powerless except God. If somebody should work to disintegrate the community, there would be a prayer to God to eliminate such a person. For someone who gossips thus causing fights among the people, the community people will sacrifice a cow to God. They address the cow, in prayer, that, "You (they mention the colour) are being sacrificed to take along with you, by spilling your blood, the dead and responsible elders to protect the living and to take away any person(s) working to destroy this community". There is also an appeal to those that cause conflict in the community to refrain or else some harm or catastrophe is looming.

One also prays to God for his problem. An old man can invoke by night over something disturbing to him. He appeals to God and may kill a cow that night. People will just get the meat in the morning. This must necessarily be something without a solution. Perhaps his son, cousin, or daughter may have had an endemic disease not curing after several attempts with possible sources of rescue. Sometimes, it may be his own making so he may plead to God to evoke his own stand, curse, or deed. Sometimes it may be normal prayer with something promised to God, (a cow and its colour specified) to offer if the victim is rescued from the disease or ailment. When there is recovery he will invite all his people, beer is made, a cow is killed and divided according to entitlement.

A dead woman without a child has sacrificed a cow but the prayers are conducted using *dura* straw not a spear. No bull or tut should be killed except her actual cow usually milked for her. But for an old man, the invocation is by spear and many cattle can be killed including his milking cows even the suckling cows with their calves.

Some four to five people can all plead to God with the spear and a designated person (sometimes the least person) will spear the animal. If he failed to kill it, another person will give it a deadly hit. When a cow is being sacrificed for a dead father, it is the uncles and village elders who pray including näär gur the maternal uncle of the dead man. The cow would be speared by his son and finished up by one of his uncles.

The most important invocation or blessing articles and instruments used in lam *Nuäärä* are: *Mut* spear instrument; rɔany *dura* straw for women; phi water; tab tobacco; liɛdh oil; cak milk; bɛl *dura*; juai grass; puɔk/ŋɛath ashes (mostly applied to guan *cölwic*); kuɔl and blood sacrifice. These are all essential in invocation and sacrifice in different situations. Loc *yaŋ* peg can be showered with water or milk. Juai grass and water phi put inside a fresh *tuɔy* guord are sprayed to the people and then the grass soaked in little water is spread on the back of the cow intended to be sacrificed. The person, who invocated, requested good health. Tobacco has definite people to administer, water is general, and grass for *Cölwic*. It is administered with ashes (wood) and if rubbed on the head, this will deprive people of rain or it may rain ahead of the person who did that. It may also be a source of water if he is thirsty. Bi ran ɛ biil ne wicdɛ bɛ *nhial* pen kiɛ bɛ dɛam nhiamdɛ.

A male calf designated to be a bull tut and had grown old should be killed on the fireplace within the compound in a celebration of all the relatives. There is an overnight feasting. All the relatives have to be informed and invited that the father's bull (he may be dead or alive) will be killed. Some of them will provide beer or food. The master of ceremonies shall peg down the tut in late evening. He is the first to start praying using the spear calling the family God that, "Let there be peace and health among people. If there is something bad in the family, (to the people) solve it peacefully". He will direct all those bad things (omens) likely to harden life. When finished he will put or lay down the spear. These articles shall be availed and put or spread on a sitting skin. A mixture of tobacco, water, grass, and kuɔl are placed on the fireplace. Water is in a gourd. The elders and" cousins of the man then pray to throw all the bad things to end with the tut. About 4 a.m. the tut would be speared by the elder son in the family. The mixture of these articles are sprinkled on this tut bull and then to the people. The tut is then speared.

Even in sickness, tab, juai, water, and *puɔgh* cow dung ashes are thrown on people as cleansing. For instance, tobacco is used by somebody possessed by a spirit or a big man mostly for illness. If the tobacco is thrown after a person going on a journey, it is a blessing or farewell with good luck. An old man can administer it as a blessing that, "You shall travel in peace to wherever you want to go. Go safe in life- no harm or danger shall encounter you". Any prayers over a cow or sacrifice using grass juai must belong to the spirit of the grass or of *cölwic*. So, the prayers are conducted using spears and grass.

Whenever there is no animal to sacrifice, kuɔl is considered as the animal of God so it would be cut provided a real animal shall be killed the sooner one is got.

Whenever people quarrelled or disagreed and was solved, the big person who resolved the issue shall spray people with water and warn them that "Do not repeat it – it is over".

If someone was struck by lightning, *Nuäär* usually advises that nobody should touch it but just throw few grass and tobacco at it. They believe the person may still be alive but once touched will die. A cow is killed, and its meat is grabbed not distributed. There is no invocation or prayers over that cow. Caa jɛ Lam ɛn *yaŋɔ*.

CHAPTER THREE
The Marriage Consummation Procedures

These practices (of rites, festivities and ceremonies enumerated earlier) are administered in different forms and at different occasions in the marriage. Although the different *Nuäär* sections have evolved different dances and marriage performances, marriage exhibits their solidarity and togetherness. This may be apparent from the booking onwards as verified by marriage procedure model one that starts forthwith, and the second model demonstrated by Nasir and Gawäär versions.

I. Marriage procedures
a. Booking the girl- *Luɔm nyal,* the initial and formal marriage commitment

When a girl has many interested suitors, then one must pay many cattle *yɔk luɔm* to book her to scare off the competitors. This usually happened whenever a prominent family is suddenly discovered to have a girl and so many families are interested to have relations with them. Hence applicants go through other sources besides the girl directly.

Because *luɔm* is a must, then marrying young man will be advised to bring the cattle to a certain designated byre- preferably the bride's paternal uncle's place. The cattle for *luɔm* booking are brought with singing, running and jumping. This booking is also waiting for the girl when she is a bit immature. Some men begin their marriages by first engaging young girls below the age of puberty. A family whose daughter is booked, the groom himself may have not many cows but wants these to nurse and multiply at the bride's residence meanwhile the girl matures. When she is to be able to be a wife, then the marriage is discussed and the *luɔm* booking cattle add to the bride-wealth. The man, in the company of his mates and sisters, plans to drive to the bride's home about five cows with at least one milking. This is *luɔm* booking. After this process the groom's father proceeds to the bride's father. Both have their relatives to explore any relations or possible bars and obstacles to the conduct of marriage that might be skipped.

This formal booking is the public announcement of the couple's intention to marry. This is an occasional call to the general public attention that a certain marriage intention is starting its process, between son and daughter of so and so families. Henceforth, people follow the other steps leading to its consummation. Some envious individuals may work discreetly to destroy or disrupt and derail such a marriage, by talking ill of either of the families. These are the ones referred to, or advised against to, 'tie-down our rumour mongers or gossipers', at the earlier part of the marriage discussions.

The marrying man and his family determine the day of betrothal or booking. They inform the bride's people that a certain number of cattle shall be driven home as booking cattle. The groom's father has 10-20 cows selected for *luɔm*.[48] These are some of the cows the father had set aside for the marriage. *Luɔm* could be four to six heifers, a bull, or two to four milking cows, which are to be

---

48   Two to four cows are usually offered for booking until the girl matured. These serve like the ring of engagement.

driven to the bride's home. Only youth, girls and women are to take them. The families of the bride and the groom are aware of the day of *luɔm* engagement. The parents inform the girl that cattle shall be brought on such a day. The bride, in turn, collects and invites other girls to be ready for this occasion. The bride's companions (girls) welcome the groom and others. The bride's mother yells, on this occasion, expressing delight and alerting the village people or passers-by, about the marriage in the process. They jump and run around. The cattle are left at the compound under the care of the bride's people. *Luɔm* is not a big occasion. No elderly person is involved it is a youth business matter or concern.

b. *Paph yiɣni* or *Määtni tuaini*. In-laws Joint Council Meeting
The first formal coming together of the two families takes place in the byre of the bride. This meeting is named *paph yiɣni* or *Määtni tuaini*. These mean 'laying of mats' or 'merging of marriage licenses' (the civet cat skins). The master of ceremonies of the bride is the one to lay down the marriage sitting mats. On this first occasion, there is only tobacco to be provided to the guests.

Määtni tuaini is joining of the two licenses and then examining possible mergers or bars to it. The *määtni tuaini* is in-laws council discussions. Each couple has a marriage council composed of relatives entitled to pay or receive bride-wealth. These two councils meet to look into marriage affairs. The *Nuäär*, like other unilineal groups, trace their genealogy descend in a lineage. They are organised into clans, whose members have a common name from which they assume common ancestry. Lineages are generally exogamous and the name is enough to indicate whether a given person is a permitted partner or not. The memory of an irregular union in one partner's ancestry is considered a disqualification. If there is relations, homicide or slight offence then it is made right mostly by the groom personally. The joint council has to confirm bars or no bars because the initial stage through children (boy and the girl) was remotely administered. Clearly, at the stage of betrothal the groom and bride, according to *Nuäär*, are *kuɔɔd* all permitted to marry and be married. Marriage for a girl is open to competition and application not based on priority or seniority. A younger girl can be married before her elder provided the latter is compensated as appeasement to bless the marriage. Her consent to the marriage of the younger sister is important. She is normally paid a cow to that effect. This is not a very serious affair.

The laying of mats or sleeping skins is concerned with bars to marriage. It is social scrutiny about the relations and families to ensure that things are clear.[49] The bride's family is duly informed when the groom's people would come for scrutiny. The bride's relatives determine when the other in-laws should come. Accordingly, the fathers of the groom and the bride, meet and decide the date, and circulate the information to their respective relatives. The groom with his companions carries the information to all their relatives that mats would be laid for in-laws on such a day. Even if the distances are far apart, the groom is obliged to give the information to all those entitled to pay the bride price. He cannot, by mistake, delegate somebody to relay the information, for this shall be attributed as neglect. Similarly, the girl (bride) informs her relatives. The representatives of the two families meet on the day and the place specified.

On the day determined for the joint meeting, the groom's father brings along his brother, friend, and other elders or age-mates from the village, probably a dozen people.[50] They come to sit with the bride's father and his relatives. The purpose of the meeting is to

---

49   Peter Kuɔŋ Wei interviewed on August 12, 2002 in Khartoum.
50   Yoanis *Ter Mut* interviewed on November 5, 2002 in Khartoum.

investigate or ascertain possible bar(s) to the proposed marriage especially homicide, relationship, and age-mate. This involves genealogical tracing and feuds to ensure that no relations or feuds could be traced. What is possible to be for *cut* compensation, either by the boy's father or the boy, all would be handled and transferred to the negotiations day.

During *määdni tuaini* any groom's person that was uttered to have offended one of the bride's people i.e. the to-be in-laws would be summoned to come along. This is for the offender to be informed or reminded about what he had committed. Actually, the marriage cannot be dissolved when the cattle have already arrived home. It is believed that if the marriage is dissolved without strong grounds, it will eventually affect the girl. She may not produce children. It is a strong rule that no cattle should be returned without a strong reason.

When the two groups are seated, after replying to greetings through their oxen names, the groom's *Jakɔk* master of ceremonies informs that, "I came to say something". He will be asked to, "Say it". He then asks, "Have I been opened the gate?" He will be *duely* answered that, "You have been opened the gate and allowed into the *luak*". The groom's master again asks his counterpart, "Is there a feud (sometimes called a 'scar'), relations or are our mats floating?" He means to ask whether their marriage is floating or hanging on a heavy bar. Although rare at this stage, if the groom is not accepted, it is assumed that a *kol* skin has been put below the mat. The bride's master may respond that, "Son of so, there is nothing. Your mat has no skin but a slight thing shall be reported to you". These are the compensations expected from torts committed by the groom's people against the would-be in-laws. With the statement that, "There is nothing", the groom master declares that, "I open the marriage with a *ruath* small bull (of this colour and age)".

Relations are traced up to 5 or 6 generations on the female side.

If the relations are 5-5 generations that is a bar but 6-5 can marry because rights cease, then.[51] It could then be concluded that this marriage has neither relations nor homicide. Then the offence or the small thing indicated earlier has to be explained in the presence of both the offender and the offended. The groom's people have to accept it at face value without discussion. Certainly, an in-law must not be told what he said is nonsense or a lie. This would be another offence to be redressed too. The slight offence is to be made right mostly by the groom personally. When these have all been cleared, the groom's people pledge to or actually pay a definite cow (colour, size and sex to be specified) in compensation.

The groom's father shall then say, "I shall go back". But then, "let us tie our dogs"[52] He is meaning that, "We tie our tongues and even if we hear bad things, we better ignore them". This is in conjunction with the *Nuäär* saying that, "In marriage, you push your stick into the grass or not raise the stick to fight. You endure everything". The message is to pay a deaf ear to rumour-mongers. Those bent on dissolving the marriage may create rumours. To safeguard against the dissolution of talks, they pledge to 'tie their dogs'. They have to ignore slanders or halt those slanders that work to evoke antagonist attitude towards the whole marriage plan. Due to people's tongue, and for fear that she might be made to change her mind, the groom could elope with the bride thus undercutting the process. This alternative situation would not be acceptable in most cases.

When there is no feud or anything to discredit the marriage, the groom's father will say, "We shall bring our cow". The bride's father would advise him where to take the cattle. The groom's father confers with his in-laws and those relatives entitled to pay cattle

---

51   See the diagram on page 21 below.
52   The dogs in this context are the rumour-mongers.

rights in bride-wealth. Any number of cattle found would be taken to the bride's parents as *cuɛc*. This *cuɛc* is actually driving of cattle which could be equivalent to engagement in another context.[53] The bride's people are given ample time probably seven days during which they prepare beer and food because there is an overnight feasting with beer, milk, food, and meat. *Cuɛc* could be ten cows. The grandparents' rights should be inclusive. They then determine when to *buɔr* wedd after *cuɛc*.

c. *Cuɛc.* Betrothal -driving home of the first installment of the bride-wealth

Cuɛc is a step to marriage. It is a man's decision to marry without hesitation. In order to speed- up or attract early marriage negotiations, he sends or pays to the bride's parents six milking cows, 8 heifers, and two bulls as the first instalment of the bride-wealth. The groom has information about the date and where to accommodate the cattle. It was determined by the father of the girl to be either his *luak* or that of his brother. The groom's family inform the bride's parents that, "We shall bring engagement cattle". This process usually starts in the evening mostly one to five days after moonrise. There is a feeling that the month of moonlight shall bless the marriage, as there would be the light that will enable cattle to be driven home. The cattle are driven to the designated bride's place from about 2 p.m. (if the destination is distant) to arrive at 6 p.m. The escorts go singing and jumping in merriment but without any *tuac* because the groom has not to go but to accompany them up to a certain distance. When the cattle arrive home they stop in front of the compound. The youth sing while the girls and young women from the bride's family yell.

The bride and her best or her brother then receive the cattle and

---

53   *Nyatik* Kuɔl Kän Interviewed on September 14, 2002 in Khartoum.

tie them down on pegs. The bride's master of ceremonies is brought to receive and ritualise the cattle by pegging them down. The bride's master would tie down one of the milking cows and throw tobacco on its peg- a sign of blessing and welcoming the cattle. An old lady, from the bride's people, will milk that cow. The master of ceremonies ritualises the cattle by pouring milk on the peg of *yaŋ billä*, on the altar, on the fireplace, on the compound, and on fireplace inside the byre. While doing so he says, "These cattle shall never be returned they are finally brought here".[54] He continues to pray calling on the God of their clan and all the things they venerate in their household. The very cousins of the bride's father must be around observing the reception. It is from this occasion that the marriage can be assessed if there is seriousness or not. The cousins then can take a milking cow each depending on the desperate ones. At this stage, the neighbours, father of the girl, and the paternal uncles of the girl would be witnesses.

The girls then receive the *cuɛc*[55] or *noŋ* who do not include the groom and his best man. Only ordinary youth and women handle this occasion. The escorts are girls, neighbours, nieces, young wives of brothers or cousins, other youths and the children who drove the cattle. These young people are all fed[56] for one night. The bride's father prepares food and milk for the *noŋ* (escorts) to consume at the neighbour's. Sometimes they can slaughter a *ruath* or ram to feed them. These youth may resist eating there. The bride's companions (girls) would give bracelets, rings or beads to induce the *noŋ* to eat food. By midnight they eat the food. During the night the groom's youth converse with and lash the girls around

---

54 This is the first formal prayer for blessing since the start of the marriage process. It reflects that the marriage is now real.
55 On this occasion of *cuɛc* they are called cuɛɛi. On other occasions they are *noŋ*-escorts.
56 Except for the groom and his best man if they were among them.

the bride. The youngest of the youth jokes with the bride. One of the boys may request exceptional services such as warm water to bathe with or special bedding, which must be provided. Surely, the wishes of the husband must be satisfied. All these are a test of the girls' ability or willingness to succumb to the husbands' demands. The escorts eat breakfast and return to their homes at 2 p.m. The village girls accompany them for quite a distance, conversing in couples or small groups. The next step is wedding, which is usually in December when there is plenty of food. It must necessarily be when the moon is in the east. The drivers of cattle, spend the night with the bride's people and a goat or a ram could be killed for them otherwise there is plenty of food, milk and oil. These are youth and so do not deserve beer. In fact, they are not expected to drink. The escorts return to the groom's father to inform him that the cattle were taken and tied down.

Henceforth, two things should happen simultaneously. The bride's father imposes some arrangements for the maintenance of his daughter. The groom's father does the same except that he cautions his son to behave himself and not dare to embarrass the family by any ulterior action of his own. These seem to be important towards the next stage of the marriage.

The first is that from this day onwards, the bride will have a special cow to feed on its milk only. The cows brought for her marriage are sacred to her so she is prohibited from having anything to do with them. The welcoming rituals performed by the master do not include her but the rest of the family. The dung of the engagement cows is set aside and heaped separately. The toothpaste for the bride must be from the neighbours, or ashes from other cows, not from those recently brought for her marriage. Her father will summon her with the mother the next morning for the following directives: (1) special diet for the girl that cow so and so should be milked for her feeding. The cow, to be milked for the girl, is specified and its milk be put in her own guord. (2) Care should be taken that the bride's eating utensils do not mix with the ones used for the cows just brought. The girl becomes a *kuud* also. She has bought ornaments for decoration such as beads, ivory armlets, clothes, beads out of ostrich eggs etc. The ivory armlets could be purchased with a calf. The boy has equally to be fattened by his parents for a *kuud* must look very healthy. If this engagement took place between April and June, *ruel* people wait till August or September when the new maize and *dura* are ready to be eaten so that the completion of marriage cattle is done. If the girl is small in age her father will say let us wait. Once she has become of age he will inform the groom's people to come for betting. But if the girl is mature the father will inform that *tuɔc* can take place within that month. But in case of a catastrophe such as death, these have to be suspended. The groom and best man determine that negotiations start in four to six days during which he will inform all his relatives and people personally-not messages.

Secondly, the groom's father cautions his son that, "The cattle are now tied pending discussion never disappoint us and don't tamper with her, if you elope with her, you shall be barred from marriage. Of course, this is a mere threat and may not affect very much if the preliminary talks were successful only remained few steps to consummate the marriage. Love marriage[57] can undercut the parents through elopement and that is still legal according to *Nuäär*. People say he has eloped with his wife. The groom's father will send information through a relative of the bride's people that he plans to call on them on such a date. If it is not convenient to the bride's family, then the information is returned that a later but

---

57   This marriage is not the skipping required steps (short cutting) but a defiance of parental consent. See p.46.

nearer day was more convenient. When the groom's father is due to leave he will summon his brother, cousin and friend to confer with the bride's people on the marriage.

There is a stage between *cuɛc* and *tuɔc* where the two fathers-in-law sit for secret discussion. The groom's father undertakes secret tipping mission *ŋɛar* to the bride's father where he is informed about the desperate and serious claimants. He will have to note the cattle rights' owners who deserve to be handled first to enable the marriage to succeed.[58] (Compensations) *cut* in marriage are trivial things. Even a false accusation of having spat saliva on some relatives is an issue to put on the table as a grudge to be considered. During this mission, the bride's father advises that the paternal grand-mother's right be brought first. Once that is done, the bride's father tells the children who brought it that "Let your father come then". When the groom's father comes he will advise him, "The maternal grandmother's milking cow be taken straight to the maternal uncles of the girl". Actually, this is the mother-in-law of the bride's father-grandmother of the bride. The bride's father sends information to his in-laws that the cow of the grandmother shall be brought on such a day (in 2-3 days' time). Two children are sent to take that cow and to spend the night there. The bride is the one to receive the cow and administer the upkeep of the *noŋ* until they (children) return the next day. The bride returns to her father's place where she would be asked about her grandmother's cow, "Have you seen that your grandmother's cow is good?" She will answer including its colour and if suckling with a male or female calf. To further show that he is serious about what should go to his mother-in-law, the bride's father would call one of his in-laws and ask him about the grandmother's cow. If that is acceptable, then that would be fine. There are cows that cannot be given out in marriage.

---

58 Peter Yieth Puy interviewed on August 21, 2002 in Khartoum.

Any cow that was partially eaten or bitten by hyena should not be given because it is believed to stamp or resemble a child. Similarly, the blind and/ or crippled cattle or of any of the colours venerated would not be accepted. *Cuɛc* is therefore over.

The groom usually gives a bracelet to the betrothed girl. She may resist but some force is used to fix it.[59] *Nuäär* believe that marriage has misfortunes that are likely to fall on either partner. This bracelet is to fend off evil spirits and protect both of them from such misfortunes.

The groom's father will instruct his son to determine the days of the wedding. It is the groom who decides the *buɔr* time. He agrees with the father and the father-in-law. The situation being clear, the groom's father says that on such a day, "the cattle shall be brought". The groom's father would send his son to a distant friend of his and the other relatives about this boy's marriage on a determined day. This is an invitation to attend the negotiations or settlement meeting. Then the groom's father will determine when he would go to the bride's father with his marriage team for negotiations, discussions and settlement. He will send information to the bride's father that they are ready.

The groom, with his best man, goes to the nearby neighbourhood[60] to inform the bride's father that the groom has come. They come to the father-in-law wearing *tuai*. They will go to the *luak* of the bride's father through the compound *cieŋ rɛi* and seat themselves on a prepared papyrus mat. The groom says, "We have been sent by the big man (his father) that the wedding should take place after two days". Sometimes the bride's father would wait to go straight for marriage negotiations rather than wedding. One of the bride's people may accept the groom's proposal of wedding. He may

---

59   Diu Kɔ̈k Warar interviewed on March 1, 2003 in Khartoum.
60   Of course there was prior information through the girl.

recommend another convenient time, probably after four days to enable him to inform and summon the bride's people of rights. The message would be returned through the same person with a definite day when they would be expected.

The groom's father will announce that he will come after a certain number of days for betting *tuɔc* and *buɔr* wedding. The betting and wedding are simultaneous. *Tuɔc* is the step of serious bride-wealth discussions and negotiations is followed by *buɔr*. Mostly youth (girls, boys and young women kaath) will bring *buɔr* and spend the night and eat there but leave in the evening the next day.

The *tuɔc* and *buɔr* are seriously organized as the most important occasions in *Nuäär* marriage. The sitting of elders over the cattle is *tuɔc* while the youth dance marking the occasion is *buɔr* are well planned. For *tuɔc* all the groom's cattle payers have to leave for the bride's place. The elders, particularly the groom's father, mothers, uncles, aunts and husbands of his sisters, go ahead to allocate the cattle by colours to those entitled on the bride's side. Relatives have rights over bride-wealth in the marriage of a girl. In the case of a boy marrying they have reciprocal obligations. The uncle (paternal and maternal), aunt (maternal and paternal) all have established rights from the girl, which cannot be increased. The uncle of the father has a cow, calf, heifer, and cow for his God and a bull. The paternal uncle has to distribute cattle among his wives according to their seniority. These elders come in the morning to attend to this business and enjoy later the beer that was early availed by the bride's people.

d. Marriage or bride-wealth negotiations: *Tuɔc*

Nuäär bride-wealth is not taken nor collected once; it is in bits commencing with *luɔm* and followed by *cuɛc*. *Tuɔc* is actually the allocation of the cattle so far availed and handed over with those still to be pledged. The binding concept is that the prospective husband should be helped by his relatives to provide the cattle wealth required by the bride's people before she could be contracted to him in marriage. The *Nuäär* term the bride-wealth as yɔɔk *kuen* marriage cattle. In the discussions, it may seem that they are discussing a price. It is claimed that the wealth is to compensate the bride's relatives for the time and trouble they took to raise their daughter-the current would-be wife to that groom's family. It is also viewed as compensation for the economic services lost or for the children she adds to the new family. Whatever is the rationale, *Nuäär* take the marriage of a girl as an uncountable value. It is like a swamp where-in one obtains fish and water foods without end. So *Nuäär* feel that closing a marriage account implies cutting off a relationship. But the relationship of affines should be one of continuing presentations and counter presentations.

Bride-wealth is never completed at once but the fathers-in-law keep a sharp eye open for an increase in their affine's stock, and take occasion to remind them of what is owed. Sometimes any sickness in a family is ascribed to the anger of the ancestors or spirits for the carelessness in paying. The bride-wealth contributes to the stability of the marriage because of the implications in case of divorce. The discussion of bride-wealth is known as *tuɔc* which is folding of the fingers in counting. The argument in this discussion, however much there may be, is about numbers and quality, how many to be paid now, how many later, and so forth. It is not a market transaction calculated on the size of herds or the total resources of the groom. Nevertheless, if marriage negotiations are likely to break-down because the bride's guardians demand more than the groom can afford, this would be humiliating to the groom's kin. To avoid this risk, the marriage broker's responsibility is recognized and thus called for. As soon as this counting and negotiations are over satisfactorily, the wedding *buɔr* follows on the same day.

For the start, the groom's people arrive at the bride's compound at approximately 10 a.m. and enter the *luak* byre in order to *tuɔc* allot the marriage cattle to the entitled rights' owners. They are welcomed by the bride's master of ceremonies for the opening session to start. Surely, he (the bride's master of ceremonies) was the one who first poured down the milk earlier on when engagement cattle were driven home. He has already prepared the sitting mats and the special seat for the bride's father. It is from this seat where the bride's father decides on whether cattle pledged are less or enough. The bride's people are seated on the left side of the gathering *luak* and ahead of them is a person designated to start the talk on their behalf.[61] The seating on the left is considered unrespectable. The respectable- the cattle owners, are to be seated on the right side of the *luak* from within when coming from outside facing the interior. The bride's master will avail a tobacco basket- a necessity for entertainment and place it in front of the fire-place facing the seat of the bride's father. There is a pole between the byre's *luak* centre and the door where the bride's father sits, a distance of almost one meter. Next to him opposite on the right side of the *luak* (from inside) is the groom's father.

The big men on the girl's side are ready and the groom's people are also ready. They are then seated as sketched in page 62 above. After greeting one by one, *Jakɔk*,[62] the bride's master of ceremonies scoops tobacco from a basket and says, "I hope you have come

---

61 He is actually the marriage broker. See the sketch on page 62.
62 *Jakɔk*- the crow is considered by *Nuäär* as the king of the birds. Any dead animal must be hit first by the crow before the other animals or birds feast on it. In its absence no other bird will do anything on it. It is the first to lay hands on after which the rest follow to eat from the carcass. So this man is likened to the crow in the *Nuäär* social affairs because he is the master of ceremonies.

100 THE PARAMETERS OF TRADITIONAL NUÄÄR MARRIAGE

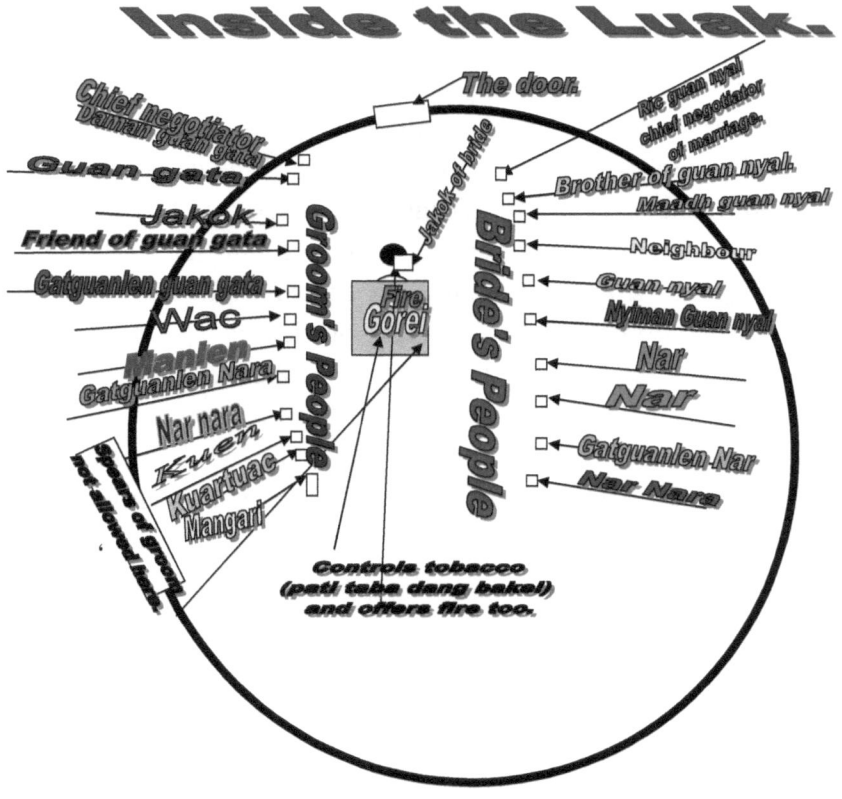

Source: Author's own drawing

due to what the children have called us to?" The groom's master of ceremonies will respond in the affirmative. The bride's *Jakɔk* will then throw tobacco behind the gɔrɛi, between gɔrɛi and the door and then on the door threshold. He has done his blessing and therefore sits. He then presents the tobacco basket to the groom's master who will in turn divide the tobacco to his people who smoke.

The groom's master says, "As we are here, tell us the spirit of your household". He means that the cattle rights have to be told to them. It is probable that the bride's people had already earmarked, or designated to those entitled relatives, the cows availed earlier for engagement. These have to be indicated to the groom's people. They (groom's people) should know by now the entitlements that are yet to be settled. The grandmother's cow on the maternal uncle's side is discussed during the in-laws' council meeting and then brought soon after. They must smoke for a while to refresh their minds before the session starts.

It is worthy of note that the fire has been heaped since morning so there is plenty of fire. A boy is assigned from the house to be responsible for and providing fire to the groom's people on request. He sits in the gɔrɛi *tiph* behind the chief negotiator.

The smoking of tobacco in *Nuäär* culture has its own flavour especially over discussion of serious matters. One takes his time to smoke and not urged to speak or respond until fully satisfied or in the mood to answer. He adjusts his mood after smoking the pipe. Even the puffing of smoke has its own rhythm in the talks. When *Nuäär* smoke a pipe, they have to feel it by using their thumbs to tamp down hot tobacco coals, though they are provided with a pipe tamper. They, instead, use the tamper to pack down the tobacco so that it burns more evenly. A pick *rib* is used to loosen the ashes in the pipe. There is a dull knife *gued* used to ream out the cake lit that builds up in the pipe. After having smoked a while, this cake is turned out on the ground as ashes to make room for more tobacco. So, the *tony* (pipe) or tobacco in general is *Nuäär* tea for the welcoming of a guest. It is assumed to be a stimulant to relieve one of fatigue as well as open the mind for fresh ideas. Hence, it is usually offered, with water, to a guest. The pipe has a significant role in marriage discussions. Apart from that, an old man marries the last young lady to serve his *tony*. She is usually called 'the wife of the pipe'. Certainly, the man has lost romance except for the one service of providing and filling his pipe with tobacco and procuring/ fetching its fire.

The bride's people then present a (bundle of grass) *ciit/juai* that sometimes contains more than fifty pieces, bound and given to the groom's people. This is the number the bride's people demand. This bundle is duly received. The groom's father asks the bride's father, "Are the cattle we brought earlier intact, or you have allocated them to rights' owners?" After taking eight or ten cows, the bride's father may answer, "Cows so and so are not earmarked". The groom's father continues to ask, "Will you give them to me or you have finished?" He will be told of those that have remained after giving sprites and friendship and paying for compensation. Of course, the bride's chief negotiator is tipped by the bride's father on his *kuth* (sprites), friends and others who deserve these types and sizes of cows, with a justification of the background to these *kuth*. So, the initial considerations are the supposed entitlements to *kuth*-(gods/sprites) for fear that these may be sidelined if taken to the last stage. In normal circumstances, no marriage discussions can break up at this stage only the rights stage. Because the bride's father is looking for properties, he will warn the marrying team that when his gods are ignored this would be disastrous because they inflict harm and kill too. These are not the actual marriage rights but outside the twenty- six cows of ideal rights. But if the bride's people did not dare to allocate them, these cattle would be returned to him in theory. They would tell him to designate those remaining. But the groom's father is strongly advised to pay first and immediately the entitlement of grandparents. The *ciit* (bundle of grass) is then offered to the groom's father after subtracting those indicated above. The groom's father allocates to the rights owners by pulling a grass (representing a cow) and setting it against a person by status. Those entitled may not like them or one right owner may reject his or hers. If cattle are few, some people will be disgruntled. Sometimes among the cattle brought earlier, there may be *yɔk jɔɔkni* cows of sprites. At this stage, the groom's father may confess that he sent them out of show (pride) and so must return them but replace them with definite cattle (size and colour).

A serious discussion ensues over those unknown or unseen cattle (yet to be collected) and those due from the groom relatives. During marriage discussions, the mother of the groom does not enter the *luak* byre because *guan luak* the byre owner- the father (her husband) is there. But the bride's mother enters the *luak*, sits behind the bride's team, to sing songs of praise and important poems for her daughter to attract and induce the groom's parents to release, give, or offer cattle. She makes much of her daughter's qualities or character but above all she is implicitly expressing the idea that the gift of a wife is something valuable. Her move is to get as many cattle as the groom's side can give without being actually impoverished.

Bride-wealth based on the *Nuäär* rights are[63] (1) Short-term marriage costs 26 cows; (2) Medium-term costs 28 cows; (3) Long-term costs 36 cows; and (4) Inflated marriage is above 37 + cows. Bride-wealth is divided between two families-the fathers and

---

63   Refer to my quantification in Appendix I A-D on pages 120-124. The bride-wealth is not ranked so but I just captured the random increase.

maternal uncles. A ghost marriage, as found in the *Nuäär* culture, is based on the right of the dead person to have a family to prosper, like the living.

Then the settlement starts with the aunt- waay. The ideal *Nuäär* marriage bride-wealth is allotted as follows: (no.1) cow for the master of ceremonies (preparation of seating) who is actually the opener of marriage discussions. This was paid or pledged during in-laws' council meeting. (no.2) Paternal unt; (no.3) bride's father; (no.4) bride's mother; (no.5) bride's father's spirit; (no.6) bride's mother's spirit; (no.7) grandfather; (no.8) grandmother; (no.9) paternal uncle; (no.10) Biel God; (no.11) maternal aunt; (nos.12+ 13) calf + *ruath* of grand paternal uncle; (nos.14+15) calf + *ruath* grandparents, man's uncles; (no.16) grandfather maternal uncle; (no.17) cow for behind the ashes; (no.18) grandmother maternal uncle; (nos.19 + 20) maternal uncle + his bull; (nos.21+22) calf +*ruath* of grandmother-maternal uncles; (nos.23 +24) calf +*ruath* of paternal uncle; (no.25)father's bull; and (no.26) bull of paternal uncle. If all these twenty- six cows are paid, they deserve a kickback *thiok* of two cows. Previously one may have offered his daughter a cow of her spirits for her to produce. This cow is kept and its offspring later becomes (kickback) - *thiok* for her daughters. So, this kickback is her original cow that used to be milked for her. Jagɛi, Dɔk and Nyuɔŋ people practise *thiok*.

It is worth remembering that both parties have some idea of resources on the one side and expectations of the other. Proce*dura*lly, the cattle offered should be displayed to the bride's kin who may reject or accept individual animals for their quality. If the bride's people were not satisfied with the cattle at hand and those pledged, they would adjourn the negotiations to the morning of the next day. The groom's relatives are advised to retreat to relax in the places pre-arranged for them so that they feast during the night. If the marriage discussions- betting supposedly went well, towards the end (actually in the afternoon) of the next day, the groom will come. The marriage team wait for the groom who should come to identify his bulls and their distribution or allotment. He has to designate the bulls for the father and the brother of the girl. Other people, in the meantime, are on the lookout, eager to see him.

The groom arrives later at 3 p.m. with the youth of his village including *mään gari* wives of his brothers, cousins, and his best man. He brings along two or three big bulls with a heifer or two. Upon reaching the front of the compound, he leaves them there under custody of the bride's people who were prepared to receive and handle them. The groom avoids passing by mid-compound and tries to enter the *luak* from the side without going by the house gate, nor amid the cattle before they are released to graze. He enters by the area where cow dung is heaped. All these restrictions are to ensure decency. Decent behaviour requires one not to just step on anything, there must be *puoc* respect. The bride's people dance in the meantime. The groom must tread on soft ground and move decently. This is where there is resistance and a struggle to snatch the groom. The groom moves back and forth to get an opportunity to throw the spear before the byre door. Actually, the spear is assigned to a fast young man to throw it and dash away lest he gets a serious beating from the girls. The youth then throw a spear before the gate of the *luak*. Once the spear is thrown the bride's companions drive the groom's friends out to the front of the compound where they both dance. This spear is a right of one of the bride's people.

The groom proceeds to the *luak* where he will allot his bulls. He enters the *luak* with his *tuac* civet cat skin tied to his waist in front. He may disagree with the cattle allotment that some in-laws combined big and small cows instead of taking either. If the in-laws were adamant, the groom, followed by his companions, would stand up, shout out his ox colour *muac*, turn the civet cat skin backwards to his buttocks and rush out of the *luak* singing. *Mi ci guan tuai duɔr loy bɛ muac kɛ thäk min cɛ kuɛan, bɛ tuac riɛt jɔkdɛ kä kacɛ rar kɛ wɛa.*

This is a protest against the way his in-laws were nagging to sever the marriage talks. By marching out he has opted to freeze the discussions and dissolve the marriage. At this point, the bride with her friends, determined to have the marriage finished amicably, would run after them, turn the *tuai* to the front and drag them back to the *luak*. This is the turn of the girls to reduce the tension and press on the elders to soften and mend the misunderstanding. The parents would not ignore this signal.[64]

Once the allotment is done to the satisfaction of all, the groom comes out soon because his sisters-in-law and the bride are waiting outside to see and dance with him. He is encircled, sung songs composed in his praise, and they flirt around with him. They continue the drill until they disperse at seven or eight o'clock at night.

e. Buɔr

During the time of *buɔr*, there is dancing where food and beer are provided. This ceremony is attended by the bride's escort, the groom's kin, neighbours, and people from the nearby villages. *Buɔr* is open and up to the groom. But *ruel* and *jiɔm* are the preferable seasons. It is during the full moon that such ceremonies can be held. If one wished to conduct his wedding, he must send information to the bride and groom's people to enable full preparation on both sides. Beer is prepared. All get informed. It must be wide information, to reach the youth, girls, age-mates, and friends from

---

64   Ezekiel Muɔn Kulaŋ (late)- interviewed on February 2, 2006 in Khartoum.

all the sides. There is pride in the festivities or hospitality. This marriage occasion is the maximum to show off.

The *buɔr* is a very important event. It is a major form of recreation and entertainment for the groom's people. Although rarely, the bride's people may say they have no means to conduct the *buɔr*.

It is then up to the groom and his parents if they wish to skip that stage and go without entertainment. If they choose to, then the groom's father will say, "The occasion should be conducted on the skin", *bɛ lat kɛ kol* meaning that his people will come with two or three women without yelling. Yelling is an announcement for attention and attendance as well. Without yelling nobody will come but people hear later that the marriage *buɔr* was done silently. But if the bride's father is prepared to conduct the *buɔr*, he will inform his relatives- mostly the cattle rights' owners of the bride, to prepare food and drinks. These refreshments are distributed according to the cattle payers too. As for all the youth, this is an opportunity to meet and make appointments. Both of them are on a show looking for future marriage partners. The spectators, of *buɔr* having seen the groom, then disperse with individual impressions about him. It is the coming of the groom that determines *buɔr*- otherwise, the elders do *tuɔc*. *Tuɔc* and *buɔr* are simultaneous. Only the wedding or marrying families remain to enjoy their meal. After the marriage is over, the elders are isolated to their pre-arranged places, probably in the neighbourhood where they would be served.

Of course, some beer is prepared for the occasion. The groom's father and his group have to consume or carry home the beer prepared and stored for them, at the neighbourhood, not in the bride's compound. There is no excuse for why they should not be entertained. Such an occasion, among the *Nuäär*, can be postponed than be held without entertainment. The bride's people entertain the groom's people. This entertainment is an obligation because *Nuäär* say the groom's people have to enjoy feasting on their cattle.

Around 6:30 p.m, the groom's people rush to break the fence of the mother-in-law, a designated part mostly right side of it. At this stage, some people jump and run. Another group will dance, run and jump with the mothers- in - law within the right side of the home compound. These are mostly the youth of the in-laws excluding the groom. They want to hear the voices of the mothers-in-law.

The youth are put aside with their women relatives. When it gets dark and all are seated, the mothers-in-law dance with the groom. This is a special dance conducted for the groom and his friends. The youth may offer the mothers-in-law a specially decorated spear as a gift. This spear is for the *duel* hut and is usually used to cut an entry into the rest house for the groom on the day of *dɔnyni cioyni*.[65] Sometimes this could be of the age-set of bride's father if this was not offered during the *cuɛc*.[66] When the mother-in-law challenges her son-in-law to dance, she would sing:

> "*My daughter is going.*
> *The one who fetches firewood,*
> *She is going. (Chorus).*
> *When she goes, who will milk the cows?*
> *She is going to her home. (Chorus).*
> *That she goes who will fetch firewood?*
> *She is going to her house". (Chorus).*

This song is called *yɔt tiär*. It is both a lament and an excitement that is compensated by the giving of *Mut riyä* the age-mate spear. Nowadays this *Mut riyä* is converted to a calf *daw* which any

---

65 This is detailed as item i on page 78.
66 *Nya*tik Kuɔl Kän interviewed on September 14, 2002 in Khartoum.

age-mate of the bride's father could take.[67] The groom is dragged or lured to the compound of the mother-in-law. The mother and sisters–in-law had already composed songs of praise for the groom. Rarely do they insult or scorn him. It is also reported that the bride could *yɔt tiär* her mother-in-law and lead her to her mother's compound singing praises for her.

f. *Luɔny tuaini* removal of civet cat skins

They dance till night after which the groom and his best man retire to have their *tuai* (civet cat skins) removed. These are skins for cattle so the girl must look for them and group into the *duel* (house) where they should be removed. So the groom and his mates retire or are isolated to a house prepared for removal of the skins. The bride with her friend must untie the civet cat skins of the groom and his best man. With difficulty, they should have the skins removed by 1 a.m. They play, beat each other, and converse throughout the night. At 4:30 or 5 a.m., the groom and his companions begin to return to their homes. It is a convention that they should not appear in broad daylight if the marriage is intact.

(i) Significance of *luɔny tuaini* civet cat skins removal

Removal of civet cat skin is a very important occasion. The civet cat skin is actually the flag of marriage. Lowering the flag of marriage signals the end of *kuɔt* the search for a bride. The girl must strive to remove the *tuai* skins, fold and roll them into a new papyrus mat to be returned after some time before *muɔt*.[68] During the process of *tuac* removal there is a strong resistance from the groom and his friend. He tries to beat the girl away from removing the *tuac*. She is likely to endure serious beatings until she has totally loosened the

---

67 Ruɔt Duɔl Rɛth was interviewed on October 9, 2006 in Bentiu.
68 Diu Kuɔk op. cit.,

tuac. If she gives up, it is an announcement of rejection of the man. The man will appear with his *tuac* on the next morning. This would be the greatest surprise to the parents. If in reality she does not like the man, she would untie the cattle and drive them to the man. She would be advised to be the only person to do that. A betrothed lady, if she changed her mind, would not dare to declare rejection of the man outright. It is probable she must have found an alternative husband who advised that the betrothal be broken up to enable him to leap into the process again. When the girl decides to break up the marriage, she will have to put on her best ornaments and perform the return and/or handing over of cattle in a full costume.

At the stage when the bride is fresh *kaw*, the groom may divorce her if he disliked what had happened. He (the groom) would sing in the compound of his in-laws and his cattle would be released to him straight away. This is an agreed divorce right from their (couple's) home and transferred to the girls' family.

Once the skins were duly removed and stored by the girls, the groom and his best man come out of the house leaving the other youth to converse with the girls of that village for the rest of the night. These remaining youth would be offered food and water.

(ii) *Yaŋ buɔr*

The next morning the *thäk buɔr* (bull for buɔr) is killed. This is the first feasting offered by the bride's people. There are no prayers when the engagement bull is being killed, so it cannot be distributed. It is eaten in one place. But that of wedding *muɔt lam kɛ* is (invoked). The youth, excluding the groom and his best man, and the women feed on it and return to their home in the evening. Of course, the elders had left by night and the groom and his best man at dawn.

(iii) Details of bride-wealth collection

Collection of marriage cattle is a deal between the groom, with those entitled, and the payers. The groom must ascertain the cattle and their colours before marriage. He collects the cattle entitlements from his relatives, assembles them, and drives them to the bride's place. The groom informed his relatives about the marriage after engaging the girl and also obtained their pledges during the *tuɔc*. If a pledged cow is rejected, it got to be changed by the payer. Whenever he found any number he would inform the in-laws to collect them. These cattle must be handed to those entitled before *muɔt nyal* wedding. Their absence would obstruct the wedding. When a sizeable number of cattle have been paid, the groom and the best man would then approach their father-in-law for his permission for *muɔt nyal* the wedding. They would be designated a day when to collect her. This is an opportunity to inform the bride's *Jakɔk* master of ceremonies for he is the one to hand over the girl and give her blessing.

The two most important stages in *Nuäär* marriage are *buɔr* and *muɔt*. They signify the end of cattle discussions and the handing over of the bride to her husband. Moreover, the most remarkable rituals are associated with these two events. Through them, the woman is fully initiated into the spear name and spirits of the household. Therefore, any lady whose marriage did not cover these steps must be re-married to fulfil them. That failing, would have an impact on the marriage of her daughters. Her daughters cannot be initiated into another household before she has been done so. The significance of this initiation is verified below.

g. *Muɔt nyal* Taking the bride.

Muɔt nyal is actually like graduating of 'gared' boys. The girl is being taken away from *bul* (dancing). This is actually the giving away of the girl. After betting, the groom's father may want to take or carry along the wife of his son. He will be told to wait because certain cattle rights remained unsettled. Once the cattle meant for the *luak* especially the father, mother, and paternal uncles are received, the groom will be told to see his mothers- in-law.

Talking to mothers-in-law *manthuyni* before taking the bride Before the *muɔt nyal* wedding, the groom and his companion go to talk to their (mothers-in-law) *manthuyni* at a place arranged by the bride's mother in her village.[69] This talking group are the groom with his best man and the mother-in-law with her friend. There is no real agenda for the discussion to explain but only to see the groom and how he talks. They may ask certain things. These are expressions of love for the groom (son-in-law). She may start by complaining that she was by-passed by the groom during the process of marriage. She may take it to be that her son-in-law does not like or rather belittle her. The groom may offer something, be it a cow, bracelet or spear, as a gift to the mother-in-law. This is a gift that the *manthuy* (mother-in-law) would give to her son in future. During this time he may also offer a spear *Mut* with which to cut the fence- an opening for his (the groom's) entry into the rest house.

On the other hand, the groom and his best friend will have to provide a goat called *dɛl pääl*. It is a *Nuäär* custom that a woman still producing while her daughter is being married must be divided with her daughter. The *dɛl pääl* must be a female goat that has never produced. It need not necessarily be their goat. The groom and friend could catch a goat while grazing and lay on the doorway of the mother's house. The goat must be laid with its right side up and the belly facing the *duel* actual house where the first sexual intercourse between the groom and bride shall take place. The mother and her husband, the groom and the bride, jump over it while entering

---

69 Peter Yiedh Puy interviewed on August 21, 2002 in Khartoum.

into and out of the hut. After this process, the goat is then let loose provided the groom brings a she-goat to the mother-in-law. When it delivers, the groom would take back the mother goat. The bride is, henceforth, prohibited from sitting on her mother's beddings unless she is suckling. If she necessarily had to sit in the hut it must be on a skin *kol*.

It is worthy to emphasize the significance of this *dɛl pääl* process. The *dɛl pääl* is the goat for leaving or abandoning the mother's beddings when the bride was weaned as a child. If this *dɛl pääl* goat were not offered, the groom would be deprived of going with his wife. The mother-in-law may refuse her daughter being taken. Moreover, if *dɛl pääl* is not procured and processed, *Nuäär* believe that the bride's mother will cease producing. *Dɛl pääl* symbolises the division of production. Once the *dɛl pääl* produced, the offspring is returned to the daughter's home. *Dɛl pääl* is relevant for a woman in production, not menopause. It serves the function of breaking incest between one and his mother-in-law.

There is a parallel convention for a young man. A young man who has matured is allowed to enter his mother's house only to fetch something but should neither sit nor carry a stick or any of the war weapons. By necessity, he can sit on a *kuicgor* (wooden pillow). If he violated or defied this, it is believed to severe the delivery of his mother. She would henceforth not give birth again because of *rual* (incest).

Having finished with the mother-in-law, the groom returns to the father-in-law in the *luak*. The father-in-law would tell them, "You can then collect your wife".[70] The groom and his best man are therefore permitted to take their wife. By this time the information had gone out that the bride would be collected. They inform their relatives accordingly. The groom's brothers and other youths,

---

70 *Nya*tik Kuɔl Kän, op. cit., interviewed on September 14, 2002 in Khartoum

without a girl, are sent to fetch the bride, at about 10 p.m. She must necessarily be taken by night because of shyness. So, the occasion is made late and the girl is kept ignorant about the timing because she may hide or run away. She normally cries. In the meantime, the bride's friends would be gathered to accompany her. They must be hiding to appear in time. No male should accompany the bride.

When they have gathered and are about to leave, the bride's father addresses them all. He calls his daughter that, " My daughter, I give you to the son of so and so..." Sometimes when the father does not trust or suspects that his daughter may not be stable in her home, he will not hurry to have all the cattle paid at once. He will remind his daughter, "I have taken their cattle so keep your home well". This advice is serious because if any divorce is initiated by the girl, her parents must consent to it. Then he turns to the groom's people. He tells them the bad things about the girl, which would require the groom to handle. She may be lazy, hot-tempered, untidy, or stubborn. The mother and father-in law caution the groom about the bride's bad cooking, and poor caring for or tending the cattle. These are issues her parents could not control but the new house is expected to force her accordingly. These are in addition to other things she will have to learn from her husband. In the end, he says, "That is the girl, you go and teach her". The bride's master of ceremonies will say, "Gentleman, she has been given to you. If ceremonies are acceptable to God, then she will produce a baby boy. When she returns to us do kill something (that is you kill an animal in the groom's place)". The bride's master throws tobacco sideways, at the bride and at the *noŋ* (groom's people) when they are leaving. This is a blessing to indicate that she has been duly released to that family. It is an affirmation of the acceptance or consent of all the parents, relatives and the ghosts of the family. The tobacco thrown after them is for her to go in peace and to prosper with children.

In this phase of the wedding, the bride leaves for her new home accompanied by girls and women from her village. This occasion of *muɔt nyal* has much force on the bride who resists and cries. She does not easily accept to go but is usually beaten into submission, by her husband's clan, to her new home. The people (escort) who have accompanied the bride stay one day at the invitation of the husband's parents. When arriving at the groom's designated house, the boys who brought her let them stay away from behind the hut. They take information home that the guests are brought. The groom has been waiting in the *luak*.

The bride and companions are standing behind the house. The groom's master throws tobacco on fireplace inside the compound, below the altar, and behind the *luak* from inside. He throws dung ashes near the altar, the main central pole in the *luak* and with tobacco and then he calls them to enter the fence.

On this occasion of *muɔt*, the bride is to be cut an entry passage between the *duel* hut and the rɛk fence.[71] When she and companions reached the compound inside the fence, the groom's mother, sister or an elderly lady in the house, would yell once at the top of her voice in happiness. This serves as an information, to all the neighbours that their wife has arrived home. After yelling the bride and companions are supposed to enter the designated house. But at the entrance to the house the ceremonial leader waits for them. He has to perform some blessings. He throws tobacco at the bride and the best man, in front of the compound, on the fire- place, then on the house doorstep, inside the house, and then rubs it on the bride's forehead, chest (breasts area) and back-between the shoulders. Thus, they enter into the house.

This special hut, in the centre of the enclosure, is where the

---

71 Abraham Cägh Riäy - a blind man knowledgeable in *Nuäär* affairs, interviewed on April 6, 2003 in Bentiu.

groom will go with the bride's companions. It is the focal point of the entire *muɔt* ceremony. Those girls who had accompanied the bride are also admitted to share in the *muɔt nyal*- the final and most sacred stage of the ritual.

When all the girls have entered the house, the groom comes out of the *luak* to join them in the house, bringing along his whips probably out of the *nyɔat* (cordial rothii tree). As the groom enters the house, the girls' companions should start to pull out or are actually beaten out except for the bride and her best friend. The girls usually strive to break the groom's whips. His brothers will lend him some through the window. Once the bride's friend is finally beaten out, the groom closes the house. He would strip off the *chip* of the bride. Consequently, she should sit down in surrender. He wrestles with the bride who resists the beating. It takes time. If the girl is tough (muscular), the friend of the groom may intrude to help knock down the girl. After that, the groom will resume lashing and the helper (man) goes out of the room. Some people would whisper to the girl, from outside, to just give in and cry rather than face unnecessary beating. Should she cry in-between, how low her voice maybe, the process ends. It is considered that she has saluted the spirits. The sisters of the man rush in to force him out. Then the groom moves out and the *noŋ* escorts return to spend the night with the bride in the same room.

Beating the bride with a small but sharp whip is, not for having done any mistake, nor for the man to show his strength but to awaken the home spirits and gods. By her midnight cry, the spirits shall know that the household has a new member. They are therefore being informed accordingly. Because "the wife belongs to the home", the spirits, being part of the household, should equally welcome the family wife. The essence of beating is for the bride to cry out and be heard by the spirits, gods, and ghosts of the groom's family.

The midnight cry symbolizes the seal of the marriage covenant incorporating her into the ethnic community of her husband. The spirits are a part of this. They have to know of the new person. The man does not utter a word when he is beating the bride. He whips out all the girls only to remain are the bride and best. After a short while, the best friend is beaten out and the bride remains alone. There may be resistance from the bride and her best friend but the groom will put up force. The groom's best man should be outside with others.

He could be by the window to hand in a few whips in case what the groom had inside got exhausted or broken up by the girl. They will be with his wife whom he beats until she cried out once at about midnight when all have slept except the 'kuth kɛ jɔɔk dial' gods and the spirits. His mother, who was hearing outside the house, will advise him to leave her. He then leaves her and comes out of the house. This is what is meant as *muɔt* without sleeping with her. But she should be dressed as a woman following this occasion.

h. Ruɣ yɔa (Yaat): Dressing the woman with skin skirts

In the early morning, before the bride is bathed in warm water, the daughter of the groom's paternal uncle takes some water, in a guord cup, and pours it on the bride's head. It is not actually washing by hand but throwing water at her. The bride then bathes by herself. While the groom's sister is throwing the water, she prays *lam* that, "You shall get old in this family and shall give birth to a baby (boy/ girl). Heavenly father, if you so wish, let her not divorce whatsoever". She is shaved of her maiden hair except for a few that are left in the middle towards the forehead for the next occasion. This shaving is a symbolic separation from her maiden normal life to womanhood. She would also be stripped of all the maiden ornaments she was wearing. These ornaments are removed, the bride is nude but should be contributed new ones by the groom's relatives. Of course she had, to leave behind, with her parents, things like dɔɔm, *guɔr* ivory armlets, döŋ, and dhuɔr, tassels duɔŋ (döŋ) ostrich eggs made into beads, to be sent for later by the groom. Should they be missing, there is a cow *yaŋ guɔri* to be paid in lieu. Nowadays these have been converted, during the marriage negotiations, to a bag and others that the groom must pay for instead.

The bride has no jewellery but only came with ornaments like headbands, ornaments, earrings, necklaces, armlets, bracelets, rings, anklets, beads and chiph- the half skirt of unmarried girls. The groom's niece, who celebrated the bathing, takes for herself and leaves the rest for the younger sisters of the groom. After being bathed and doused in butter oil, liɛdh *yaŋ* the most familiar form of cosmetic among the *Nuäär*, the bride is then dressed, with *yaat* a woman skirt made of skin, by the niece of the groom.[72] Alternatively, the bride is dressed in a contemporary fashionable garment. Here ends the function of the niece and so she goes out of the room. After this function the bride is called '*kaw*'. She is of course a woman *ciek* but would preferably be considered (newly wedded) *kaw*. Her real womanhood is after cooking or giving birth in her new house. Though she had not yet gone with her husband, if she were to run away right after this, she would be remarried as a *kë*, second hand woman.

(i) *Yaŋ muɔt*

In the meantime, the accompanying girls will clean the groom's compound including the three or more neighbours so that people know that wedding is taking place or a bride is being wedded in that home. At 7 a.m. the groom's father brings a *ruath thak* small bull. It is for ritual and so has to be tied on a *Nyɔat cordia rothii*

---

[72] She is related by descent not of the actual paternal uncle.

peg hammered down by the groom's master on the right side in the compound of the *luak*. Its colour must be identified. The girl's companions may reject it, if it is so small, and demand that a bigger ox be provided and slaughtered instead. But if the girls accept it, people are asked to sit on mats prepared for the occasion. The groom and best friend sit in front while the bride and her best friend sit on the other side facing them. They are then regrouped to sit on one row, from left to right, the groom and bride, best and best, groom's mother and father all sit. This small bull is to be sacrificed but invoked by the groom's father or uncle, or master of ceremonies including other elders from the village and those invited on this occasion or for the purpose.

The groom's master of ceremonies plugs a hair[73] from top of the bride's head *yuɔt*[74] *miɛm* and either throws it to the peg or holds it with the spear during prayers. It is a custom that a woman whose *miɛm* hair was not plugged out, cannot partake in the *Nuäär* ritual prayers, except through her small child who will be given *puɔgh* cow dung ashes to throw. She can hold onto his hand, like when swearing, and throw with him together. The plugging of the hair is of the first lady who will later have a say in that family. To exert herself she would refer to that act in contesting any opinion in general. This is welding or mending of the production of the two families. The hair *yuɔt* plugging signifies the removal of maidenhood and

---

73 In olden days a bride would be shaved with a few hairs, called *yuɔt*, left in the middle of her head. It is the *yuɔt* that should be plugged out in the groom's home. But in case she was not shaved, the groom's master must pull some hair from her head.

74 *Yuɔt* is also applied to those being 'gared' for guan theɣni dien to plug out when he is going to lie down. It is assumed that ci gar bi kai, the 'gar' will not burst. There is also *yuɔt* for jul. Jul is a child who survived after three or four dead brothers or sisters. When such a child is shaved a yust has to be left including its mother. According to Thomas Kumɛ *tɛkɛ yuɔt* jul`. Jul *tɛkɛ yuɔt* me ba pal wicdɛ kɛnɛ wic man.

preparing her for a new growth. This is like gar initiation, and she is told that, "you shall produce in this household". This action has been the initiation of the functions and prayers.

(ii) Advices and safeguards to the newlywed couple.

An individual family is happy and satisfied with the marriage of their children when they are seen progressing well. The newlywed couple are usually given advices or counselled in another way. Elders talk to them telling them the rules by which they are to live from now on. Sometimes these elders give straightforward instructions and admonition to the couple mixed with insults or given in a form that conveys it. Through such advices, the roles and expectations of the new couple are geared to opportunities of success in life. However, they are advised to cope with family stresses and tensions, and are made more conscious of the disadvantages of divorce. The couple are told that family breakdown would have an enormous damage on the development of their children. The children shall have improper growth or upbringing.

Some of the couple's potential problems may emanate from the groom's parents, the groom or the bride. These should be prayed *lam* against. The father of the groom may tip those he invited to *lam* to touch on the issues he dislikes from his wife. He may just open or close the *lam* but leave the rest to the other elders. What these elders stress are mostly advices on how the couple should live decently. The couples are immunized against disappointment and despair in life. The groom is charged with full responsibility for that lady and to observe family matters. Any of his usual shortcomings are declared or confessed publicly and advised against. These are secrets of the groom that must be related to his wife, by the father on this occasion, so that she would adjust to her husband.

Proce*dura*lly, the groom's master starts the ceremony. He is the one to peg and tie-down, and to start *lam* the prayers on the *yaŋ muɔt* wedding bull. The master pulls hair from the groom's head and mixes it with tobacco, *dura*, maize seeds, grass, other seeds of trees and rice. These are all put in a small cup of gourd with some water. Each celebrant uses this mixture by scooping from it, pours on the peg and throws to the cow, the groom, to the bride and all over. All the talks and invocations would be addressed to the bride, the groom, the father and the mother of the groom, the cow being sacrificed and then God. When the groom's master finishes, he lays down the spear. Someone to pray then picks it up, sprinkles water from that mixture and speaks. In that sequence the spear is put down and picked by whoever was to pray.

For the start, the groom's master picks the spear, holds it together with the hair and grass, and prays pointing the spear at the cow. In lam he addresses first the bride that, "Lady, you have been brought to this home, do I kill this cow?" She must consent publicly before the process proceeds. The master is concerned with rules. So, he wants to ascertain that the girl accepts that the animal be killed as binding of the covenant. It has to be confirmed that she likes the household. This is the last of several occasions where she has the opportunity to back out or say publicly that she agrees to the marriage. She would always make the appropriate gesture. It is worth noting that some girls forced into such marriages later run away before *dɔnyni cioɣni (*going with the man). But when she accepts or consents to the killing of the animal, it is believed that its blood shall haunt her if she ran away. Most advices to the bride are additions to the ones given her by the parents. When the bride is going to her house, her parents advise her against biting a man if they fight. She must not urinate in bed. These are mistakes once committed have to be paid for by the parents.

In the second place, the master will confess all the bad things he knows about the groom's mother. He addresses her that, "The wife of your son is handed to you. You are going to divorce her because of the bad things that you do. You are troublesome and have bad behaviour. These will make this girl run away. Take care; the blood of this cow will haunt you".

The master looks at the groom's father and says, "You will leave your wife to destroy this new couple! If you allow that to happen, then, what will you be in this household?" He turns to the bride, "That is your father, and mother-in-law, take good care of them. Right from today, you take your pot and cook for them. Whenever your mother-in-law offended you, accuse her to your father-in-law.

We concur with your father who gave you to me. You will give birth to a baby boy in this household. You are now a wife of the family".

The groom is advised by the master that, "You (mentions his name or oxen colour) the daughter of that nice, honourable and hard-working family is now given to you whole heartedly. Even the spirits and ghosts of this household have accepted her. Because you are lazy, troublesome and disrespectful, you and your mother are going to mistreat, neglect and make her run away from this family. You know very well that no one in this household is known for such things. You are now responsible, leave those bad practices and take care of your wife and the children God will give you". The master ends here and puts down the spear.

All those elders to lam follow this pattern, until the groom's father or paternal uncle concludes it. The old men of the village took it in turn to deliver long speeches, gesticulating with the spear to mark their points. They spoke rather angrily in a gruff voice. During all this *lam* there is a general call and imploration of the ancestral spirits for protection and good health. The celebrants pray for peace and riches in the household.

When the groom's father speaks *lam* addressing his wife, he is actually advising her, implicitly, to leave the couple alone to make their own life worthy of living together. Probably the mother had almost no means of influencing the choice of her son's spouse. She was duty bound to submit fully to the decisions of her husband. She may slander the bride to the neighbours. If the groom's mother had commented adversely on her son's fiancé during the marriage process, she would be cautioned not to invoke an antagonistic or hostile relation between the girl and her husband.

The groom's father takes over with further advices to the bride that, "Your mother-in-law is not a good lady. If you are not patient she will have you divorced. So I agree with your parents who prayed for you and offered you to us. We are agreed that you shall first produce a boy". The father may end here to let his brother conclude and spear the cow.

The bull being sacrificed is patted on the back and also addressed. The groom's father or uncle says to the bull, "You are not killed for malicious intentions but for peace, harmony and prosperity in this household and this new home. So this occasion is to consummate the marriage which should be cemented by giving birth to a male baby called after you (colour of the bull)". The groom's father or uncle only spears the cow. It is to be skinned by someone else.

The groom's master takes the spear strained with the blood. Earlier on, he plugged the groom's and the bride's hairs mixed them with tobacco, grass, and water contained in a cup of guord. The spear used for killing the sacrificial beast is dipped in that mixture, left in the cup of guord, and rubbed on the groom's and bride's feet, chest, breast, head, and back between the shoulders. This is a further blessing and cementing of relations.

In this *lam* even the dead ancestors are addressed. This takes the form of conversational monologue without repetition. They speak to the dead as if they are addressing a living person face on. The words combine complaints, scolding, sometimes anger for neglect, and sometimes appeal for forgiveness. But in this marriage occasion, the dead are also informed of the event, pleas are made for their approval, efforts to ensure success for the marriage and the children that will be born to it.

When the cow is slaughtered, the people and all the youth, who conversed together last night, return to eat in the huts. The carcass is carefully skinned, cut up and divided among the members of the bride's clan. The meat is all carried off, to special people *ji cuŋni* (the people of rights), except the head and the *larco* that are to remain in the house. Chest is the right of the maternal uncle. Previously, the inner parts would be washed and boiled lightly to avoid rotting and carried also. But these are nowadays to be cooked for the escorts. At 2 p.m. the youth are sent to distribute the meat. The tail, which is made up of fat, is presented to the bride's father. It is cut with a good piece of meat as the right of the age-set of the bride's father. The tail is a very important part because it is eaten on its own occasion. All the age-mates of the bride's father are called to eat it in one place. Sometimes beer could be provided.

As for the bride, she would be returned, by 4 p.m., to her parents' home by the young men, girls and young women. These *noŋ* carriers or escorts spend the night at the bride's place. The bride's parents shall slaughter a ram or make good food as super for the *noŋ* so that they spend the night conversing and, of course, being satisfied. They return to their homes the next morning, after eating breakfast. When the bride is thus returned home, her parents shall offer her a house where her husband could visit her and step on her feet. *Nuäär* describe the first sexual intercourse, between a bride and a groom, as *dɔnyni cioyni ciek* "stepping on the feet of the woman".

In the afternoon of that day when the *noŋ* returned, the groom comes with his best man to the in-laws after initial information through the neighbours. They have come, bringing along the *dɛl pääl*, to cut the entry gate for the night later. The mother-in-law with another lady must be sitting inside the fence in the direction where the opening has to be made. An opening is made by the groom and he enters with his best man and the goat. The goat is handed to the mother-in-law. It is then laid on the doorstep held by the women inside for the father and mother-in-law to stepover into the hut. The groom and best follow suit. However, they come out and proceed back home only to return by night later. The goat is taken to the *luak* or let lose if it was somebody else's. The mother-in-law makes the door for this special entrance.

i. *Dɔnyni cioɣni ciek.* Stepping on the feet of the woman

Nuäär people have no misgivings about the physical relationship between men and women. Though sex is a mystery, most couples understood almost something of male-female sexual relationships when they are married. Therefore, *Nuäär* youth went into marriage expecting that nature will simply take its course and children would be born. Among the *Nuäär* sex is meant for reproduction not for enjoyment or gratification. They hardly talk directly about sexual intercourse. To speak directly is bad manners reflecting disrespect. There are implicit terms that describe it such as ca *ciek* (*nyal*) dhɔm, a woman (girl) was raped (ambushed) ca böŋ, she was knocked down, cɛ cioɣ *ciek* dɔany he stepped on the woman's feet, cikɛ tɔi kɛnɛ *nyal* he slept with the girl.

After the wedding *muɔt nyal* the groom and the bride cohabit in a place prepared by the bride's parents. The groom will start leaving their home at 8.p.m that day going to the bride's place and arrive probably at 10 p.m. He moves dressed in his leopard or civet cat skin. If he arrived earlier, he has to put up or wait nearby. If his presence was not felt, he has to throw a stone to fall near the house for the people to hear. This signal is for the bride's people to go to bed earlier. There is an opening cut on the fence behind the house. This is the groom's secret entry gate. He then enters the fence leaving behind the spears. The woman would fetch the spears and bring them into the room. He will spend the night with his wife but must leave by 4 a.m. He should not oversleep as to be seen. Of course, during those days when the people were naked (nude), it was an unpleasant scene to see a groom. Even the movement of a woman, known to have had sexual intercourse with a man (her husband), was restricted. However, premarital sex surely existed, but no woman who indulged could talk about it because she would be considered promiscuous. She would try to avoid being seen because of shame or shyness for having lost her virginity. The *kaw* bride had instructions from the mother to awaken her husband at the first cockcrow. To ensure that her husband has gone, she must stay outside within the house compound to enable the father, mother, and other elderly parents to come out. Sometimes her mother would make some movement around the hut, signalling that it was approaching daybreak, hence they should come out or disperse. So, the groom has not to appear but sneak out of the house early. It would, therefore, be a big shame as well as bad behaviour against the bride's father. The groom would have been disrespectful to his in-laws and may be penalized for that.

At dawn, she provides some water for the man to wash after which he moves out with his *tuac* already tied around his waist. The bride carries the spears and hands them to him after being out of the fence behind the hut for a very short while. At a distance, out of the site of the in-laws, the groom would untie the skin, hang it on his shoulders and proceed to his home. The significance of *tuac* is that at the in-laws, this is an official costume. Moreover, the father-in-law can summon him for a consultation anytime.

But should his father-in-law want to talk to him, he will inform his daughter (the bride). The groom will, in the next day or so, appear at home wearing the civet cat skin he used during his marriage. This is the only occasion where he could be seen at home in broad daylight. At about 8 a.m he will be summoned to the *luak* after the cattle have been brought out and the dung removed. He meets his father-in-law and they converse after which he will be told what he is wanted for. After their discussion or meeting, the groom will proceed to their house for the rest of the day. He can't spend the day in-doors at the in-law's place without eating. Moreover, he would be a nuisance to the in-laws because they would be extra careful with his presence. Their talking and normal way of handling things would be restricted by the "presence of the groom in the house". All in the family would be made to know and note that. The presence of the son-in-law, or cɔu *nyi*ŋu the husband of the daughter, imposes another protocol. So, this is when he could be seen and people know that his father-in-law requested him for a meeting. If the initiative for a talk is from the groom, he will inform his wife to coordinate with the father-in-law. The groom will come during the day with his *tuac* on according to the agreed time and day. He departs sooner the issue of the message is over.

The husband visits his wife regularly. He passes only the night with her but living and working during the day in his parents' homestead. He makes longer but regular visits, their *dura*tion depending primarily on the distance between the villages. If the distance is considerable, the husband might visit his wife once every two days, spending one or two other days in his homestead. He continues visiting his wife in this way until she has conceived. In the old days, the bride remained with her parents and may travel to her home for the weaning of the first child. But nowadays, it is two to three months after which the bride is requested to attend to and be full time in her home. While, the groom comes to the bride's place he doesn't eat there. The rules of social conduct prohibit him from eating in his father-in-law's presence, particularly during the first years of marriage or until he is expressly invited to do so. There has to be a formal invitation for the in-laws to eat together. A ram or small bull is usually offered for one to eat and/or drink water at or with the in-laws.

j. *Ba nyal wicdɛ luɔc jɔk. Mään-* womanhood stage: a step before she cooks

After the bride got introduced and initiated into the family she would return to her parents' home. When she decided to head back to the groom's house after two to three months, this is the stage of *mään-* womanhood. This is a programme that has to be implemented. It is her mother(s) who determine/decide to undertake this procedure. Her father could be informed later. Some *dura* has to be pounded for her with beer made and milk. All her relatives have to be informed that the girl would head back to her husband's people, which implies all have to contribute milk or beer in big pots. She has to be accompanied by her relatives, mostly her sisters, cousins, nieces and nephews to carry these food items. Of course, some information should have gone to her in-laws when she would head to the home. The arrival time is usually 6-7 p.m. The man's people feast on milk and beer. Prior to this occasion the girl, or the bride, could work with her in-laws but hardly eat there. That evening when these foods are brought, she won't eat. She could do that at her parents' home before coming. In the next morning, food shall be prepared by her husband's parents/people and not from what she brought the other day. It is cooked in her house. Before she eats it, she will have to scoop a spoonful and put on *tut duel* doorstep of the house, *wic buurä* on the windscreen and then she can eat after that. Henceforth, she could come to do some job for a day or days and return to her parents' home. She could spend up to a year with her parents so that *puoc*dɛ shyness fades gradually and gets integrated into her household. Gradually she gets acquainted and understands them.

II. Other condensed versions of Nuäär marriage stages
a. The Nasir Version[75]

About the age of twelve, a boy is due for initiation-scarification, to manhood. *Gat me ci run kɛ wäy kä wäl rɛu ci gäri du thiak.* He will ask his father, "Am I not big enough to be marked now?" *Bi gur thiec „ Ɣän kan dit kɛ ɣo de ɣä gar?"* The father may answer that he was still. The boy is bound to wait for scarification until his father consents. Of course, the father wanted to ensure that his son has reached the stage of self-reliance and could be responsible for others.

Dɔŋ bɛ we ŋöti kɛ kuë.A mäni me wɛ ji jiok ci ku dit ba ji gar. Once the boy is marked he is confined to a house for some time as a *chɔt*. When discharged from that confinement his father gives him a stick and a spear- stools which he didn't have to own as a boy. In case the father did not offer him, the maternal uncle will provide them.

The young man continues to court girls for five years or so. Should he be the elder son, his father will inform him that he is now responsible enough to have a home- a wife, of his own. This is the *käm kuen* stage.

With that license the young man goes around looking and asking

---

75 This was related by Joseph Tut Jɔak from Gajiok section belonging to *cieŋ Nyali*eth in Malɔu area. He is 50 years old. He was interviewed on January 29, 2007 in Juba. This was later confirmed by twelve others in the acknowledgement. Accordingly, the Nasir version goes thus.

for a nice girl. If he bumped on one he will report to his father that he found a girl by such name from the family of so and so and belonging to such clan. He would seek the opinion of his father. If his father has a fair knowledge of that family, he could say that the father of that household is his age-mate or that family *"thilɛ kɛ dieny"* have no basket meaning that they give birth to few. Accordingly, they cannot marry them. In the alternative should that family have a history of an evil eye, or incestuous relations, the boy's father will advise against having an offspring from people of such background. This is the *Dorcieŋ* stage of tracing any vices in that family. But if that family are hard-working, not father's age-mate, no known incest, and no homicide, he will send his son back to inform the girl that she is acceptable to this family.

In the meantime, *bi kuud/kuen* (the would-be groom) should report to the girl that no marriage bar was found by his father. The girl shall also reply that her father in the *luak* too consented to the initiation of marriage procedures. So, she would let the young man know that he is accepted for further arrangements. He should go home. Immediately, the young man would ask when he, in the company, could come back. She would fix the next day as convenient for them to come. On that day the young man with his mates come singing around 8 p.m. They seek to be assured of their love *thiec nhok* stage. They spend the night singing, joking and conversing in the hut designated for the marriage. The girl and the man stay awake throughout the night. The girl and her friend lean against the wall on the right side of the hut. The girl's head is covered with a cloth. The man and his best friend would also sit on the other side. There are spokespersons *Jakɔk* on both sides. The two spokespersons sit in the middle between the two groups. A certain girl is assigned to keep the fire lighting has not to quench. The groom's spokesperson would offer his counterpart some money as an opener for talks.

The bride's best lady could be her niece who has been married and probably given birth so that she can talk vigilantly i.e. not afraid. The spokesperson of the bride receives the money and declares *kuanɛ ruac* that "we can now talk." Then she would proceed to ask, "What are you talking about"? *Bɛ thiec i "min lat yɛnɛ ɛ ŋu?"* "We came for marriage" would be the answer from the groom's side. *Bi Jakɔk wutä we "bä nɛi a la kuen"*. But "who is marrying among you?" The best man would say Mr. So and Miss So, She would reply that, "Okay we have accepted you we shall forward you (with your case) to the parents - father in the *luak* tomorrow."

A while before they are invited and led to the *luak*, the young men have to come out of the hut and wait behind the *luak* in the field. Around 7 a.m. the young men are to be seated in the *luak*. The lady chief of ceremony would prepare the sitting mats in the *luak* before she invites the youth to enter. She would inform her elders to attend to the occasion in the *luak*. Once all have been done, the lady in charge goes to the young men to guide them to the *luak*. The youth come and one of them keeps singing until they are seated inside. Not to distract the attention of the people, no children or women are allowed around. The spokesperson of the youth will address the bride's elders, "Fathers, I have come with interest to talk to you." *Ɛn Jakɔk luak bɛ we "guaari, yän cä ben gorä ruac kɛ yiɛɣ"* He puts something on the skin/mat before them. The bride elders call themselves by bull names. One of them is asked to take control of the discussion. *Dit nyal ba rodiɛn ner i "dhuɔr ŋu", ba we "dhuɔr ŋu jin bi ruac kɛ ciɛŋ nyadu."* The person delegated says, "you sons of.... (to be addressed in his bull name) this small girl brought your case up. She has accepted you and so do we. We may disagree over the cattle issue in the *luak*. We found no bar to marriage." The youth spokesperson would respond immediately that "we shall bring our ring after tomorrow." The elders would advise that "we give it three days." *Ba kɛ jiok "muɔcɛ jɛ nin daŋ diɔk."* Coming out of the *luak* one of the youth starts singing. Of course, the girls are waiting outside to see them off to their home accompanying them to a certain distance. Nearing their home, one of them will burst in singing. They are heard and welcomed by their people and all singing and jumping in happiness till the groom's father's *luak*. The father asks if they have been accepted and they reply in the affirmative. With that response, the father instructs his son to take preliminarily four to five cows or even 12 for a rich person including a big bull *thak*. After three days those cattle would be taken by the groom accompanied by boys, girls, and two men to enjoy drinks for the youth entertainment, and two women who would sing.

This stage is a combination of *luɔm, yɔat wec nyal* and *cuɛc*. This procession *noŋ* starts jumping and singing as from 3 o'clock meanwhile those cattle of *luɔm/cuɛc* are being dragged by the boys. They must necessarily arrive at the destination- the *luak* of the paternal uncle of the girl, at sunset. The children are seated and cattle are pegged down. In the meantime, the youth are directed to their designated house. Ba cɔu *nyal* jiok "wɛa *duel*un bi wä nyur thin." By about 7, 8 or 9 p.m a small bull is slaughtered for the youth to feast on throughout the night till the morning. They offer the bride's father some meat- usually *hoi*. One woman among their group *noŋ* would be given *lɛat* meat to share with her mates in the group. There should at least be two or three milking cows within the *luɔm/cuɛc* cattle. The girl's paternal uncle shall send one milking cow to his brother- father of the girl. In the afternoon, the *noŋ* have to return to their home to arrive at night.

If the bride is mature, the groom's father will urge that he settles the marriage gorä yo bä *kuen* pik. Accordingly, he will send a message to his colleague (father of the girl) on the other side that,

"I want to finish the fire of that calf of the other time." *Bɛ guanthu gatdɛ jäkä ran i «Ɛn dɔw e dan gorä yo bä macdɛ be thuk."* Normal marriage ranges between 22 and 30 cows- *piek kuen (tuɔc)*. He may send the groom with his friend that, "go and sleep in the wedding/ marriage house and inform your father-in-law that I want to settle your marriage." *Wëniɛnɛ duel kuen bi thök lar guthudu i gat ŋu gorɛ yo ba kuendä be lat.* The bride's father may give permission for him to come after four days. *"Gat ŋu a bäk kɛ kɔr nini daŋ ŋuan."*

Within this period some beer and food shall be prepared. The bride's father will summon his relatives (those with cattle entitlements in the marriage) and friends for the occasion. Some of them may help with food or beer. The groom's father will come with all his people to enjoy the meal and drinks of the occasion. When he arrives he will ask for the bride. He will be welcomed and offered *ciet/juac* the bundle of grass numbering the cattle being requested. The bundle is untied and counted, and the number indicates the total cattle entitlements. The groom's father sets aside a number of grass meaning the cattle he has at hand and says, "This number is within my ability for the moment. As for this much that should pend until we see if we can't be offered the girl. *Juai titi a liph- bä ca jek mi ba muɔt nyal pen ɛkɛn.* The bundle accepted will be apportioned to all the persons entitled including friendship right. Those unsettled cattle rights are called *töc jɔr*- remote sources. Those sources could be girls' that are yet to be married and entitlements, once obtained, from them will be ferried to this marriage in the future. To be specific he could say that his niece called so is being married and he will get the maternal uncle's right soon. Once availed, he would use it to settle the remaining cattle. Alternatively, the bridegroom's father may have grain to sell from which proceeds he can buy cattle. He may point to an outstanding debt he owes someone and hopes to get it soon. Therefore, *yaŋ* a dud "the cow is in the grass."

From here only remained the big marriage drum that people play as from 2 p.m. But *tuɔc* starts about noon and has to finish between 6 and 7 p.m. so that there is time to feast on the beer and the food prepared earlier. During *buɔr (ŋut)* if the bride's father is wealthy or proud, he may kill a cow on this occasion.

Early next morning the bride's father would offer the marriage bull in honour of his daughter who is departing from the house.

Nyadɛ min jiɛi ni cieŋdɛ- thiɛgɛ nyadɛ. It is tied down and the bride's uncle (paternal) says that "you call her out I have something to ask." *Bi guanlendɛ we "cɔalɛ nyiŋu tɛkɛ mi bä ben thiec ni jɛ."*

All her brothers and sisters should be around. When she attends, she would be told," The marriage is over only remaining you. This bull is going to be sacrificed now. Have you really taken this gentleman as your husband? *"Jin kuen cɛ thuɔk ci duɔdh jin, yaŋ bä näk thi-eckɛ ne ji, dhol ɛmɛ ciɛ nhɔk?"* She would answer that "I have not withdrawn just collect your cattle." *"Kan kac jɔk gorɛ ni yɔk kun."* Out of excitement her brother starts to sing while shooting into the air. The whole group run around yelling and singing. It is the turn of the bride's father to pray. He addresses all the gods saying "what we and the groom's family agreed, let this girl go in peace and to form another clan over there. She will give birth to a boy. Therefore, you the god of this household and that of the groom's confer to accept and bless this marriage. This girl came to us about this case through the *luak* in broad daylight– not conceived or eloped." *Bi guani nyal lam jiokɛ kuth i "mɛ ca mat kɔn ji cieŋɛ kɛ ji gɔal wutä ni mi, nyamɛ a jɛ wä dor cak bɛ kai kɛ dhɔl. Jin köth cieŋɛ kɛ köth cieŋi maatɛ. Nyal cɛ ben kɛ thök luak kɛ cäŋdär."* Soon after this the bull is slaughtered, skinned and the meat is laid on the skin. The groom's father then instructs his son[76] to distribute *buath*

---

76   All that the groom does is to point at the meat using his stick and is picked and given out to those designated.

kɛ riŋ the meat as follows: *Lët* goes to the groom's girls. *Yoi* and the head should remain on the skin for the bride's father. With all the distribution over, the oil for the god- usually hang inside above the door of the *luak*, is brought out to anoint the bride with. She would be anointed – breasts and behind the shoulders and the hands. Once that is finished the bride's people would say "our arrangements are over you are free to determine the wedding of your wife. Whenever you ask we shall give her to you." *Bi pek nyal we "ci ruacda thuɔk muɔt ciekdu bi lat yɛn cäŋɔ bia thiec ni jɛ mɔ bakɔ jɛ kam yiey."*

When the groom is ready, he will come with two men straight to the marriage hut and ask for permission to enter the *luak* the next morning. Obviously, they would not be denied an audience with the father -in -law. Seated before the father-in-law, they inform him that "we came to take our wife." The bride's father also informs them that "we have wound up since that day. What remains is your concern with your mothers-in-law." After this they go away. Sometimes they may choose to spend the rest of the day in the village to confer with the mothers-in-law. Alternatively, they may go back home and appoint a certain day where they would avail the entitlements of mothers specially spears and money. The mothers complain that they have no cattle rights in the *luak*. *"Thilɛ kɔ yɔɔk luak"*. Therefore, the bride and companions offer those things inside the marriage hut. They are then told "we have given you your wife." *Ba kɛ jiok "Ca kɔ yɛ thoph ciekdun."* The *muɔt nyal* has a small bull or goat to be given by the groom. The bride has a few (8-10) days to look for other companions. Their number may be 50 girls because some may be *yɔac* (volunteers dragging) and others are *noŋ* (escorts). The family of the boy would avail a lot of food, meat, and milk. The *noŋ/yɔac* of the bride can loot the whole village with impunity. They grab any edible things.

(i) *Noŋ and Muɔt Nyal*

The bride is usually taken to her home at dawn and not before 2 a.m. Once she arrived in the morning, a cow would be killed by the father of the boy who will pray that- "The God of this house-hold, be informed that the son --- has married let him create another clan." *Köth cieŋ ɛmɛ, ŋak cɛ kuɛn, a je nyɔk dor dɔdien kɛ cak."* Around 4 p.m. that same day the bride and her maiden are brought out to sit on a mat in front of the mother-in-law's hut between the door (halfway from it) and *buɔr*. The niece of the groom removes the bride's cloth, shaves her hair and gives her brace leases, beads and white earrings etc. She has to be stripped of the maiden ornaments, contributed more decorations and tied a new skin skirt. The chiefs of ceremonies of the groom then anoint her with oil same as done earlier by her parents. This is followed by women and girls yelling and singing. Once this is finished, they resort to their designated residence. The bride is due to leave with *noŋ* during the following day. The groom can follow after three days and put up in the earlier marriage hut. In case, he wants to dignify thiɛk *cieŋ tuacdɛ* his in-laws, they will have to do some hoeing for some time. His companions have to be allotted another hut. Although the groom has his own room, after hoeing, he has to bathe and eat in the house of one of his nieces married in or near that village. That mission accomplished, the groom goes back to their home. After some time the bride's parents may ask her to visit her home with a few girls (10). *Cieŋ nyal ba nyadien jiok, "lɛni wä guel cieŋ du naŋ nyiŋu kɛnɛ nyiŋu bia wäy."*

This group carry along with them some beer, alcohol, and milk in gourds as *puɔdh* that must be eaten by the whole village. When receiving such niceties, the father of the groom may even kill a bull for this group of bride. Otherwise, he could do a better one than that. Hence, that is why *Nuäär* say that marriage is a *tuɔc kuen ɛ* töc swamp that is endless and full of many good things. Sometimes the father-in-law could be offered a cow by the groom as an invitation home. That animal is to be slaughtered for the father-in-law to feast on with his age-mates. This occasion marked the end of the respect of not sharing certain services in common. Henceforth, the groom can eat, drink and mix freely with his father-in-law *ci thek cu thil.*

(ii) *Nuäär* Nasir marriage entitlements
- När Kui *luak* (5 cows), Mandɛ (3 cows- *yaŋ*-dau-*ruath*).
- Wai- liac (one cow).
- Manlen- one cow.
- Dɔaŋni-mandɛ (one cow) ; guandɛ (one cow).
- Däman *nyal*- Thäk (kɛdä- of his stick).
- *Määdh*- one cow (liac).
- *Yaŋ* pal- man *nyal*.
- Kuth- man; guan.
- Cuŋ Näärä kɛ *nyi*muɔr me ci dɔŋ, kɛ *nya*mi ci liu.

While the bride has been with her parents until she delivered and the child is due for weaning, she would go with the child finally to her home and only visit her parents casually. Now her parents say our daughter has to be taken home *nyaŋadi ba dhuɔl cieŋ*. She is provided with plenty of food for her settlement in the new home. She has to start cooking with the help of the sisters of her husband. Meanwhile, the child has to be taken back to the grand mother. A milking cow is offered for his/her care (weaning cow). The bride eats outside the house with *mancɔadɛ* sisters of her husband. The sisters *mancɔadɛ* of the man may conspire that he catches the woman eating so that her shyness disappears. They do that because when they leave her to tender her own house, she would have no alternative except to take vigilance and handle food for her husband.

b. The Gawäär Version of Nuäär marriage[77]

The scarification long ago was 18-19 years after puberty. The elder son would be given responsibility for the family wealth- cattle. He has to drive the cattle to the seasonal camps while courting girls at the same time. He leads the cattle to burned up grass and drives them to the river late in the evening. He may remain to enjoy dancing but for some time. If he has become mature and strong enough to fight and sleep with women and there are some cattle, his father will authorise/licence and direct him to search for a nice lady. *Bi guan ɛ jiok "ci kam kuen gori."* Once he got one, he informs his father that "I found the daughter of so and she accepted *nhɔk*[78] me." *Nya ŋu cä jek cakɔ ruac kɔnɛ jɛ.* Should his father know that man perfectly, he will ascertain that the daughter of Mr... "What did she tell you?" *Nya ŋuŋa- nya dhuɔr ŋu? Cɛ ji jiok i di?* From such a question the groom can deduce that his father would favour the marriage. The groom will answer that he talked with her and was accepted. On the other hand, the girl had also informed her father in the same manner. The consent is sent back respectively by each spouse. The search for the qualities and bars to marriage are explored secretly and reciprocally.

The youth leave on a certain day for a rendezvous under a tree near the bride's area to meet the girls there. This stage is *luɔm kuen*. Each side selected a team leader *rui/Jakɔk*. These are the spokespersons to manage and guide the talks and conversations. The dialogue is opened by the groom's team leader who addresses the girls that, "this mission is for your sake. For acquaintance introduce your names all one by one." Each *Jakɔk* introduces all

---

77   This was related by 50 year-old Yoanis Puɔk Kuic. He is a Gawar from *cieŋ Nya*ng of Jithep. On February 2, 2007 he was interviewed in Juba and counter checked with other Gawäär and Fangak people who are indicated in the acknowledgement. Their version is indicated thus.

78   *Nhok* in *Nuäär* has both meanings of love and acceptance/agreed to.

the companions by names. With the introduction over they move to the agenda. The youth team leader says "we came for marriage." The girls leader may respond that "we have accepted *nhɔk* you." As soon as the answer is heard, the youth leader says "my function is over" *Cä`thuɔy*. He then addresses the groom that "Mr... there is something else that you can ask. *"Dhuɔr ŋu, jɛn a kɛ mia ci duɔdh nä bi ku thiec ɛ jin.* The groom will just want her to confess and confirm what they had earlier discussed by saying "Your leader told my team leader that you have accepted *nhɔk* us is that true?" *Jakɔkdu cɛ Jakɔkdä jiok i cia kɔ nhɔk- ɛ kac kiɛ ɛ waŋ?"* The bride will confirm that "If I did not accept *nhɔk* it my sister (leader) would tell you nothing. I accept it." *Mi kan jɛ nhɔk, thilɛ mi de lat ɛ nyimar- yän cä`nhɔy.* The groom soon bursts in singing. There is an immediate request to take the marriage to *luak*.

It is worth noting that the bride's elders are already assembled in the *luak* for the occasion (outcome of the youth discussions). The bride's team leader goes to inform her fathers in the *luak* that "we[79] have been courted *luɔm* and we have accepted them as our husbands." *Bi Jakɔk nyal guani jiok luak i "ca kɔ löm kä cakɔ kɛ nhɔk kɛn cɔwkɔ."* She would be told to let them come. *a kɛ bey.* The *luɔm* were waiting for the elders' response through the bride's *Jakɔk*. While waiting for the groom and his group, the bride's relatives move with their group to right side of the *luak*. The groom's team-composed of the groom and two others (his leader and one other person) sit on left side of the *luak*. The *luɔm* were waiting for the elders' response throughthe bride's *Jakɔk*. The team leader of the groom is greeted through his father's bull or name by his father's age-mate. Either they greet one by one or all of them by mere show of hand. The groom leader addresses the elders that "father there is

---

79   This is the royal 'we' because it is only one person wanting to marry not all of them.

a talk between us and your daughter. We are coming to tell you that we want your daughter for marriage relations. Were you informed about that?" By this stage, *tuai* have been taken to the *luak*. It is the turn of the bride's father to ask if they were accepted by the girl. *Kä ɛn nyal cɛ yɛ nhɔk?* The answer would be positive. They would be told that "what you heard from our daughters we also accept it." *Ɛn ruai min cia liŋ kä nyiekɔ a mäni kɔn bä cakɔ yɛ nhɔk.* Out of joy the groom sings. The bride's elder says that "we have accepted you just determine your days. *Jakɔk guan nyal bɛ we "Kɔn cakɔ yɛ nhɔk kuë duŋdun möc nin"*. If the groom is ready with cattle, he offers a short time. Of course there could be other young men interested in the girl who could work to derail the marriage. But this depends on the bride's parents who have to prepare refreshments. However, the groom would say that we shall bring home our calf.[80] *Bakɔ dawda muɔn cieŋ*. Regarding this step the bride's elders advise the groom's team to pull out for consultations while the bride's people do the same. *Wërar cɔu nyieti, wëŋërɛ kä bakɔ ŋër.* They would all confe a convenient date. The groom would be told to bring their cow home after three (3) days. *Kuëyaŋ-dun muɔn cieŋ kɛ kɔr nini daŋ diɔk.* Of course it is the two Jakɔak who have conferred and agreed. With this they are bid farewell and reminded to bring their cow home after three days. *Kuëwe mal bia yaŋdun muɔn cieŋ kɛ kɔr nini daŋ diɔk.*

They move out of the *luak* with the groom singing. They proceed to where they left the other companions. Of course, it was the groom plus two others who had to talk to the bride's elders. The girls then accompany them home up to a reasonably long distance. The girls bid them farewell and ask when they would return. *Bi nyier kɛ jiok "gati kuëwe mal. Bia ben i nɛi?".* The

---

[80] No *Nuäär* man will ever say the number of his cattle. He would lump all of his cattle as a daw *yaŋ* calf.

youth answer that they would return after two days and on the third day they bring the cow home. *Bakɔ ben kɛ kɔr niini daŋ rɛu. Kɛ diɔk diɛn bakɔ duŋda noŋ cieŋ.* Once at home the groom charges people with his *tuac* tied to his waist. Soon they inform the parents and relatives that they will take their cattle home after three days. The groom's leader informs the father that "we have been accepted and we told them that after three days we shall take our cow home." *Kɔn cakɔ nhɔk. Cakɔ kɛ möc nin daŋ diɔk bakɔ mun ni yaŋ cieŋ.* The counting should start from the next day. The father confirms what he has heard so far. After eating some food at the groom's, the youth then disperse to their homes. The father then confers with his son over the number and types of cows to take.

They may decide that there should be 4 milking cows, 3 expecting cows, and 2 bulls. The father would indicate/designate which cows to go. He could send for his intimate cousin to explain to him that his boy has been accepted by daughters of so and so. The youth are going to take the cow home and the elders shall follow with the *tuac* to the *luak*. His cousin will answer positively. *Gɔa dhuɔr ŋu.*

At the appointed time, the young men alone shall take those cattle by night. They should start at 5 p.m. and arrive at 7 p.m. They go silently without singing *noŋkɛ yɔk kɛ luud- thil tuar.* These young men would be received by the girls. There is a hut prepared for these grooms *cɔw nyiet.* If the bride's father wants to show off- or be proud of his daughter, he would slaughter a bull for these *noŋ*. They spend the night in that house and could also be offered food. Since they are sons-in-law and not the groom they can eat in the house. The girls and the young men converse throughout the night. The cow slaughtered on the spot is to be skinned and the tail *juäl* should be carried, that same night by the son of the bride's father with two others, to the groom's father. Of course, the groom and his best man cannot eat there. If this were a harvest time, all those youth would clear *ŋer* the *dura* of the whole village while they are feasting on their bull. This could take them one or two weeks to finish the harvest. They are then free to return to their own village.

(i) Määtni tuaini

The groom's father will invite his age mates to enjoy the tail brought to him. This is to show them that the youth who took the cow home were slaughtered a bull and the tail is brought to us to feast on. After their feasting, the groom's father would send a word to bride's father that they go after a day or two to confer on the marriage *banɛ tuai ben maat*. Their discussions start with the question of homicide. If there is nothing then they comment on what the children have brought before them. Then they say it is good so far. The groom's father would say how he had wished to be related to the bride's father if he got this opportunity. Now is the occasion to talk over the issue. *Gɔa ciɛ mi jiek yän gorä maru ni me thile guath mi jekä ne jɛ. Mi ca töy ɛn nyamɛ kɛnɛ dhɔlɛ gɔaɛ ber banɛ ben lat*. Of course, beer is in plenty with meat. They eat, drink and discuss freely. Everything going well, the groom's father says "we shall come but regarding that cow brought home earlier, it shall be *tuɔc* not *buɔr*. It is *tuɔc* in silence *tuɔc kɛ muathmuath*. So, the bride's father prepares his *juai* grass bundle. Since a cow has been taken to the bride's home, it is apparent that other desperate applicants may intrude. So *tuɔc* should take place instantly. Based on the above circumstances, the bride's father may open *tuɔc*. Bɛ cu we *tuɔcnɛ*. Also, this *tuɔc* is in silence cikɛ *tuɔc* kɛ muathmuath.

(ii) Buɔr

Even if the public were not informed, they just proceed with it on that the information would come later. The bride's master of ceremonies would say "let us then discuss." The groom's father will pay as many cattle as possible. After this, they agree on the date for *buɔr*. Before cattle could be scarce or few the bride-wealth used to be 50 but this had dwindled to 26-15. Both agree to conduct *buɔr* in the next 6-8 days, so that information does not go out fast, otherwise earlier is better to avoid overcrowding which might provoke fighting. All the relatives would be informed that on such a day we shall go for *buɔr*. They usually have to arrive at 2 p.m., singing and shouting. The youth groom included, have to drive the cattle to the bride's *luak*. All the pegs and the whole compound were stripped clean. The elders follow slowly and could be there by 3 p.m. and proceed to the *luak* where they find the bride's elders already seated. A lot of beer is served to these elders, but the youth have to consume theirs at night later. The bride and her maiden have to prepare sleeping places for her mothers-in-law, according to ages where they would be served their meals and drinks. The old mothers stay with their husbands.

(iii) Luɔny tuaini

At 8 p.m. the groom and his youth are taken into the house. The groom has his *tuac* on the waist. Fire is kept lighting in the house and they converse. The bride (her head covered) is sitting with her maid and opposite is the groom and his best man. Between them in the middle of the house are the other youth. The groom's master of ceremonies would address the girl's *Jakɔk* that it is already night let the fire be lit *ci yɔu la wär ba mac pɛt*. There would be a strong resistance to that because instantly the *tuac* has to be removed by force. The bride with *guan tuaide* should come and have it removed - strip the man naked, the girl would be forced to see the secret part of the man. The *tuac* is in reverse order. The girl will untie the *tuac* with difficulty. There is a struggle (by the girls) to have the *tuac* untied in darkness, but youth want it in the light. While the youth are engaged in the untying process, the elders are enjoying their beer. Once untied, the *tuac* is thrown to the bride's companion who would then roll it. The bride would be stripped of that cloth (veil) and she would resort to their place with her friend. Henceforth, food would be served to all except for the bridegroom and their friends.

The young men struggle to quinch the fire to sip the beer without being seen by the girls. If the congregation was large then many spend the night sitting otherwise, if few, then there is an opportunity to sleep. The groom and the bride go out in the field while the best man and the maiden also converse somewhere outside. A little before sunrise they come back to the house. *Cɔu nyal bikɛ wäy wuɔth kayni kɛnɛ ciekdɛ. Ji tuai daŋ rɛu bi muɔŋ rar ɛn thɔŋɔ. Me ci yɔu baak bikɛ löc duel.*

(iv) Tuɔc

In the morning people assemble in the *luak*. Of course, it has been cleaned and people enter at 9 a.m. They all line-up accordingly and start to *tuɔc*. The masters do the business with the fathers. When all have been settled, the groom comes to allot his bulls. The betting and consultations alternate to consummate the occasion well. As the process continues, the bride's father may kill another cow for the marriage people to feast on. The bride's parents will say, "We shall look for the rest of the cattle in due course as for now we shall give you your wife."

The groom's master of ceremonies sings, *tuar, muai* and then calls upon their spear saying, "Let her firstborn be a girl so that she pays back these cattle." *A jɛ kai kɛ nyadɛ kɛ yo bɛ yɔk luɔc jɔg.* The bride's master follows in singing and saying, "our spear, we have given out this girl if you accept she should give birth to a boy to take over the power of this household." *Bi guan buodhni nyal tuar bɛ we "muda nyaamɛ cakɔ jɛ thoph. Mi nhɔgi jɛ a jɛ kai kɛ dhɔl kɛ yo bi mac cieŋ ɛmɔ mal te tetä dɛ."* They spend the day in the house waiting for the cow to be slaughtered at 4 p.m. The people are seated outside the *luak* compound. People pray over the cow *ba yaŋ lam* and the evocations of the *luak* are repeated. The bride's father would inform his daughter that "I have given you to the son of so even if he gave me no cow, I just want his relations. I am going to kill this cow on the basis in which you brought it. Do you still love him? I am going to kill this cow." *Ci kam gat ŋuŋa cäŋ thilɛ yaŋ mi cɛ kam yä cɛ gor ɛn yo bakɔ mar. Jin yaŋ ɛmɛ bɛ näy kɛ pek e noŋi ne jɛ. Ɖötɛ kɛ mi nhɔgi jɛ? Ɣän yaŋ ɛmɛ bɛ näy?.* The daughter would say "I have not changed my mind just kill the cow." *Ɛ ne ruac e dan thilɛ mi cä cay. Yaŋ näyɛ.* He then turns to the groom saying "Son of so, you have made us- we your fathers, to sit this long, is your intension intact or have you changed your mind? *Gatŋu me cikɔ jakä nyuɔrkɔ kɔn guri, ɛn me dan ŋötɛ thin kiɛ tɛkɛ me ci cay?* The groom replies that he had not changed his mind. *Thilɛ mi cä cay näy ni yaŋ.* He then says let the cow be slaughtered. The animal is then slaughtered. People spend the night again. They leave the next day carrying the remaining meat to their homes.

(v) *Muɔt nyal*

The bride's father informs the groom to take his wife after two to three days. Bia *ciek*dun be kɛ kɔr nini daŋ 2-3. After that, the youth come to fetch her with *noŋ* at about 8 p.m. and may arrive at 6 a.m. at the groom's place. The groom's father kills a bull - *yaŋ noŋ*ni. The masters of the groom's ceremonies have to pray a little but not so much evocation and the cow is killed. All the *noŋ* are fed except the bride and groom. The bride is taken to a designated place where her hair is shaved except for a strip of hair *yuɔt* left in the middle of the head. The groom's master of ceremonies or his nieces can plug out the *yuɔt* hair. By night the bride is dressed in a leather skirt by the sisters of the groom. The groom then enters the house to beat her *duäc (teŋ tuɔr)*. Of course, the groom had prepared earlier on some straws as whips to clean the dust off the bride *yɔti bɛ tur ciekdɛ tɛŋ*. He will leave her as soon as he has exhausted the straws for lashing. Or alternatively, his mates may call out on him to pull off her *dhuɔri put dhurɛ*. After this the bride is, returned to their home where her husband would step on her feet *ba cioykɛ wä dɔany ɛ cɔwdɛ*.

The groom is expected any time after 8 p.m. so all the family have to be indoors about or by that time. If his mother-in-law is still producing/giving birth i.e. not menopause, he has to enter the house wearing one shoe on the right foot. If his foot has no shoe then he has stopped his mother-in-law from producing. *Mi ŋöt manthuydɛ kɛ dap bɛ ben kɛ war kɛl-pek cuei. Mi thil cioykɛ war, cɛ manthuydɛ ŋöy dabä*. This procedure is applicable to the elder daughter *Këy*.

(vi) Cuŋ Kuen Marriage rights/entitlements among the Gawäär

Pek Guan
1. Guan *nyal- yaŋ* dhurä, *yaŋ* gɔarɛi, *yaŋ* buath, daw billä, *yaŋ* mandɔŋ, *yaŋ* guandɔŋ, *yaŋ* määdhdɛ
2. Guanleen mandɛ-*yaŋ*, daw kɛ thäk guanleen.
3. Guanleen kuɛi*luak*- *yaŋ*.
4. Wai mandɛ- *yaŋ* (daw me *guɔr* rɛu).
5. Wai kuɛi*luak*-daw.
6. Man *nyal- yaŋ*.
7. Däman *nyal yaŋ* kɛ thäk.

Pek Närä
1. Näär mandɛ- *yaŋ* me lar, *yaŋ* mandɔŋ- lar/liac.
2. När kui*luak- yaŋ* me lar/liac; *yaŋ* guandɔŋ; *waŋ*nen- ru-ath kiɛ daw, dɔŋ mantuti -*ruath*.

These two models are singly featured by much interaction between the groom and his father-in-law as compared to or contrasted with the western *Nuäär* model. Some steps in the original seem condensed and shortened in the last two modifications. In essence, there isn't any significant difference as long as the marriage entitlements are maintained. The rituals and festivities are also observed with emphasis sometimes .

CHAPTER FOUR
Establishment of a Home

A home starts with an abode followed by the other essential things that serve to identify it. Construction or identification of a house, where the woman cooks, and the shrines – altar *Riäk* and *buɔr*, are erected and the woman gives birth. Her children are named according to the circumstances of the family and the elder who initiates the name. This sums up what the home entails. This household is not expected to dissolve through divorce. We shall elaborate if the covenant (marriage) of this household can elapse or not.

I. Housing

The elementary family does not become an independent domestic group soon after the stage of the wedding. It is only when the spouse established their own household that they begin to be economically independent of their parents' households. A bride receives from her mother foodstuffs crockery, furniture and other household requisites. Besides the pots and other utensils given by her own mother, the bride also receives from her mother-in-law some items necessary for her household. These are usually a millstone, a flat wicker basket and a large earthenware waterpot. If the groom's father is rich, he may give his son three or four cows at the establishment of a home. A husband will have set up his own homestead, prior to *tuac*-giving, starting with a single hut in which he and his wife will live.

For a young man, home is where one stays with ancestral relatives, in-laws and friends. It is the emotional and physical place where one learned, from childhood, about the traditions, morality, and the form of creed or belief one's forbearers lived by. People build houses to provide themselves with a sense of place, personal identity, and privacy. An individual's house *cieŋ* kiɛ dhɔr ŋu is one of the important visible symbols whereby he can display his wealth and position. Housing is closely linked to the way in which families are organised.

A new family does not constitute an independent domestic group.[81] This interdependency may be broken on the initiative of the groom's parents, who may suggest that their son should establish his own field in their village. Work on the field is usually done cooperatively, the husband assists the members of his wife's household for a certain time in their field and then they assist him in his, which is usually small.

For a newly married girl *kaw*, if there is a *luak* being constructed by the groom's father or brother, she considers it her *luak*. It has to be erected with poles, bamboos, straw, cane, and plastered. These building materials are to be collected and put in one place. She will be responsible to collect the grass, bundle and tie them in heaps, and carry them home. She has to bring the byre poles that have been cut down in the forest. Some are spread out on the ground, and others are erected or held up where they would be found. The *kaw*

---

81 William Gai Chaŋ interviewed on February 8, 2003 in Khartoum. Berkeley, Los Angeles, London, 1996, p.225.

bride will enrol the assistance of her younger unmarried sisters, brothers, and nephews. The groom's in-laws may help. The bride's father may take the responsibility of thatching it. The mothers-in-law help in plastering such new buildings.

Establishment of a home starts with a house and then *luak* follows. The man is the head of the household. He does the hoeing and brings food. Due to all these, he is likened to a peg until his wife becomes menopausal with big children. She stops herself from the man alone. She then looks after her children and hoes a lot to bring them up. She would not care much nor worry about her husband. If they have cattle, she would convince her husband to marry a young wife to nurse him. As she has given birth to several children she is elevated to the status of gatguanlendɛ a cousin. She is understandably old enough to be neither admonished nor beaten vigorously but can assert her opinions forcefully and openly against her husband.[82]

Hence, the home, in this context, is that place a man with a girl he married must stay in. They could be offered an established place or erect and construct their own. Their stay is to be prepared by the groom's people. The bride's people have a different role according to *Nuäär* traditions. For instance, among the *Nyuɔŋ Nuäär* people, *thiok* of four (4) milking cows are usually paid to a groom for having settled most of the cattle entitlements. This is a kick back to enable the groom and bride to establish a new home. The bride's people pay it on the basis that their daughter has nothing to settle with. If it is denied, or not paid, the marriage cannot break nor dissolve because it is the pride of the bride's people. It used not to be a right for the groom to ask for kick back. But the man may create problems for his wife that would force her parents to reward him each time for trivial problems between him and his wife. He

---

82 Sharon E. Hutchinson, *Nuer* Dilemmas, University of California Press,

may magnify trivial problems in order to be compensated. Hence, the kickback is offered to appease him.

Some married couples do not move away immediately but instead build a hut for themselves in the homestead of the groom's parents. The homestead is thus expanded by the addition of another hut and shelter. It usually has a separate entrance to the yard and is separated from the rest of the homestead by a fence. Every family becomes an independent economic unit even though it may live, for the time being, in the homestead of the parents. The young family cultivates its own fields and has its own livestock, and the wife now cooks for her husband and the children of the household.

For a new harvest to be eaten, *dura* or maize for the twins must be cut off the ground from the roots. This should be carried ahead of the compound and thrown there where the birds shall feast on it. If it is collected and eaten by the boys, it is assumed eaten by the birds. When the *dura* is ripe and harvested, the white crow comes, followed by a bird called *luɛtluɛt*, and then *jɔw yier* another bird. When all these have come and are seen, people then conclude that it is the end of the rainy season. The food for twins is made *koph*, the beer for twins is brewed, and this year's *dura* straws are burnt. This is an indication that the new harvest is over and ritualised for consumption after these things have been done. All these are done so that twins do not *nuer* (contaminate) when they eat the new harvest. During winter, people bring cattle out of *luak* and the *biɛl* beer is brewed, sprayed out and then drank.

II. The bride's initial cooking: *That Ciek*

The groom's father goes to his counterpart (bride's father) to request that the wife of his son be released to them because they are in desperate need of her assistance. Of course, the bride often went to her house and did all sorts of things except cooking. She was not yet entrusted such responsibility but could also eat there and spend a day or two. So, when her father accepted the request, she would be made ready. The bride's father would call his wife and inform her that, "Our daughter shall go to her home, prepare yourselves". The mother would offer a small girl to accompany and help her at home. She will be provided with some food. Then she will be selected *kuay* (utensils), food, oil, dishes and spoons for her husband, father-in-law, and mother-in-law. Some women who know cooking and home maintenance shall be availed. The *kaw* sends information to the groom's people that "We shall come on such a day". When they arrive to the groom's home, usually at sunset, the mother receives them. She has to call her husband that "The mothers-in-law of so (the son) have come home". They are welcomed, seated and a ram is slaughtered without prayers. There may be a mother-in-law, amongst them, who should not drink nor eat in this house. She has to be taken to the neighbourhood. The groom shall have informed his age-mates and those elder and younger to him, including neighbours and age-mates of his father. The groom looks for his walking mates from the various places to attend this occasion.

The bride does not cook upon coming to her home. It is not spontaneous but should undertake a process. In that morning when the *kaw* (bride) should start cooking, an old lady would come, mostly the wife of the groom's master of ceremonies. The old woman fills a (pot) *cuy* with water and puts on two (stones) *dool* against the *buɔr* (windscreen). The *cuy* and *dool* all are new but *buɔr* should be plastered or renewed. The old woman would put down the pot and return it up. This process is repeated three times. While in this process, the old woman is actually praying solemnly[83] pleading to the stones that, "My stones, this woman, who has come

---

83   *Nya*kual Kɔy (died) interviewed on May 6, 2003 in Khartoum.

here to this house I give to these stones, and she should remain here". This prayer is in line with the general *lam* only that she does not talk loudly. After the third time she makes fire and says to the bride, "Wife of my son, you can now cook, those are your stones". She scoops water with *liɛr* a new cup of gourd and sprinkles it to the door of the house, *buɔr*, the bride, fire, the pot on the stones, and the fence gate. Again, she says, "Wife of my son, my stones which you now inherit or take over, you shall grow old in them here and never shall you abandon them", and so she proceeds. The cooking initiation process of the bride has been conducted. The bride is thus authorised to cook. The occasion's sacrifice is the male elders function to perform. Meanwhile, the bride's other sisters do the cleaning of the compounds, fetching water, bringing firewood, cooking and all sorts of domestic work. The whole byre compound is cleaned including those homes neighbouring this *luak* (at least one on each side). The dung in those homes is collected and removed to leave the *luak* clean. The companions of the bride anoint with oil the children of the house including the neighbours.

The bride puts the food on the fire already prepared. She is not to prepare this initial meal wholly alone. Her companions, the other girls and women, have to help or teach her in the process. The bride observes how they are cooking because she will have to continue on her own soon after this meal. When the food is ready, it is put into dishes tög and mixed with oil. The people eat around tables or rows of age-mates. The table or row itself now becomes the focus of the home and the place of companionship. The meal has a less boring structure and sequence. The meal together is a reunion with old friends and the making of some new ones. It gathered people scattered across long distances. This is more than consumption for nourishment's sake. The community way of life is eating, drinking and feasting together. In the context of time, place and the people involved, that cooking is a focal practice. It is therefore one of the mediums whereby lives are centered, ordered, and sustained. The meal cooked is certainly the stuff of moral community. It has a centering and orienting force.

The food cooked on this occasion is to be tasted first by the nephew (son of the groom's sister). He is the one to clear the *piy* (wood for stirring the food). The nephew scoops food and puts it on the *buɔr* to cool. Then he removes the food on the *buɔr* and eats it. Some part of the food is made into "tëŋ".[84] The woman, who first initiated the cooking, shall avail and fill *thääy daŋ rɛu* two earth dishes as *tëŋ* for the children. There are twelve other dishes *tög* to be prepared. Six go to the groom's mother with her age-mates and daughters. The other six go to people of the *luak*- the father and his sons. The food that remained in the cooking pot is given some oil and milk for any of the groom's sisters. Each group distributes according to their ages, numbers and sizes. The people of *luak* can distribute the dishes thus: Three dishes *tög diɔk* are for the groom's father (even if dead) to eat with his age-mates including younger and elder to him. The groom and his brothers have three dishes too. The old women seated in the house are the groom's mother, her age-mates, her daughters, the neighbours, groom's paternal grandmother, and all the children have a dish each. Initially, four dishes are to be filled first: one for the father, the mother, the groom and the brothers. Then follow the dish for neighbours, sisters of the groom, dish for the groom's paternal grandmother and others. Of course, all the food has oil and milk.

The dishes are then distributed to their rightful owners, by the nephew, the bride and her sisters, and the master. The bride brings

---

[84] The top of the cooked food is usually given to children who must be sitting around. It seems a custom that this part of food must always be eaten by a child.

food, milk and spoons to the *luak*. The food is to be distributed to all those therein. There are three rows. The first row is of the father and his companions. The second row is the groom. The third row is groom's brothers. The youth sit on the right side of the *luak* and men are seated before the gɔrɛi, on the left side of the *luak* in front of the fireplace. Inside the *luak* facing the people, the bride goes on her knees and puts the big dish covered with päät. The spoons are placed on the päät. She places it in front of them. She returns or goes back crawling and get up at the door of the *luak*. She brings milk with her sisters. The fathers' *diar* milk guord is placed before him. The bride's sister takes the other *diar* for the groom.

Before eating the real meal the new wife had already prepared, the master of ceremonies brings the food, scoops and eats it. The master carries the groom's *diar*, pours milk on tut *luak*, altar, inside the *luak* at *thiriɛu*-the tallest pole to the tip of the *luak* and leaves the *diar* there. He comes back to fetch the second *diar*, scratches the groom's food and puts in milk. He summons the groom and best and the bride and best to sit before him. He scoops some food and pours on tut *luak*, gɔrɛi and that is all. He scoops the food with spoon and orders the groom and best to open their mouths and gives each a mouthful. He does the same to the bride. It is the production of two families being united or webbed together. Many people are in the *luak* watching the events and there is shyness because sometimes the children laugh or mock at the spouses and the bests. The master addresses the bride that, "My daughter, it is this food that you shall quarrel over with your husband. This shyness shall fade away and fighting begins". After this, the master gives up the feeding of the bride and groom. The groom and best, and the bride and best are not all going to eat from this food. Some food has been made for them at the neighbourhood. The rest of the people eat according to their distribution. This is all the meal for the morning.

The *laagh tögni* literally means the washing of dishes but it is a metaphor for super on this occasion. The evening food or super is only for the old people- mostly the groom's father and mother and their friends. They eat it throughout the night and also drink beer, provided by the bride's family, to help in food digestion. The children, girls and women, who accompanied the bride to this cooking occasion, shall return with all the *kuay* utensils they had brought along. These exclude the ones allotted to the bride by her mother. The groom's father may, out of happiness, say that, "The in-laws of my son are broke". He will offer a cow, preferably milking, to be taken to the bride's father. For the *noŋ* a ram dɛl could be slaughtered for them to eat for breakfast. They are free to collect any remaining meat to their homes. These cases are optional gestures and are a show-off than a requirement.

This very house where she cooked must belong to her and if it originally belonged to the mother, she might be built another place. When there is no erected *buɔr* one is to be made. This *buɔr* is actually the centre of the house- altar for the woman. Only nephews climb or sit on it. When a husband divorced a wife (by ill intend), the wife will curse that "If you divorce me maliciously, just to enable you marry another wife, unless I was not the first to erect these stones, I doubt that that woman shall make this house any good". If she was wrongly divorced surely the new wife will either not produce at all or her child shall die. From this time the woman will identify with her house. If she is asked whether she came from their house or her house, she would proudly say from her house.

A bride normally starts cooking in *ruel* or jiɔm. When she started to cook in *ruel* her husband may eat with her in jiɔm. This is not actual eating from one dish but be able to detect and see or watch her eating. Otherwise, he will hardly know when and where she eats in the home. It is only when the man discovered or caught her eating that they are assumed to have eaten together. The bride is usually afraid to eat much so some people have to force or encourage her to eat.

From now on, the groom has to behave like a married person. He should note that he has thus moved from the warrior class to a married life, family. A married *Nuäär* man can go to a fight but not to spearhead problems. He does not cause trouble because he has become responsible. If he has children, he should not wish to be blamed for acting as such. He can start or ignit troubles normally, with his age-mates but not with lower or elder generation. He will not frequent *bul* (dances) because he has married and is not a youth. The girls, who used to look upon him, will give him up because they no longer see him as a potential groom.

III. Erection of household shrine

With the house established and officially taken over by the housewife, the essential things associated with the home are the *buɔr* windscreen and the altar *Riäk*. Both are focal symbols when sacrificing and in invocation. Such ritual centers make up the opulence of the house. There are some rituals associated with a shrine that are private and secret. Others are family ceremonies. Every *Nuäär* household has one or more shrines devoted to the purpose of rituals and ceremonies. The construction of *buɔr* is not an occasion worth consideration. But once erected, to repair or replace it need some ritual. The altar is put up once. It is used frequently. Both the *buɔr* windscreen and the altar *Riäk* are used occasionally as reflected below.

a. *Buɔɔr*

Windscreen buɔɔr is like the woman's altar. It is right in the center of the hut compound därthök. The children sit around it watching and waiting for the food being cooked. In normal circumstances, the children converse and sleep there before moving to the room. The *wicgɔal* serves the same function for the elder males of the family. Beer is poured on it by old men- mostly master of ceremonies. He does it as to the *luak*. A woman's beer, being consumed by wives of age-mates of her husband, must be poured on buɔɔr, thök *duel*, and thar*duel*. When the newly married woman erects her buɔɔr it is not an occasion to celebrate. But once erected it serves as altar for the woman. Small children and the unmarried *cɔw caŋ* (brothers-in-law), whom she found at home not yet ear marked, can sit on it. If it is spoiled and deserved repair or is broken down, it has to be spread on the ground by the nephew, son of her husband's sister. It is then made and plastered.

The fireplace *wicgɔal* or *gɔrɛi* (central hearth in the compound or inside the byre) and the windscreen are for warmth. They are also a focus, a hearth, and a place that gathers the members of the household from work and leisure. Both are locations that give the home a center. They engage their members. Duties are assigned and responsibility is learned. Tasks are appointed and skills are acquired with them. The conversation is carried on together. They enjoy one another's company. The fairy tales, werewolves, and marbles are conducted here. With all of these, the children's character is formed and shaped. Thus, the fireplace has a communal moral dimension.

b. *Riäk altar*
Every household has one or more shrines devoted to the purpose of rituals and ceremonies. The opulence of a house is often referred to in terms of the number of such ritual centers, it possesses. The rituals associated with a shrine are not family ceremonies but are private and secret.

Riäk is actually the (altar of the family spirit) *biɛl diedhdu* ciəŋdun. *Riäk* (altar) is made of *Nyɔat* (cordia rothii). Any cow being killed for sacrifice has to be tied and pegged on a *Nyɔat*. Cow of the spirit of biɛl of the household head, and bull of the man must all be pegged on *Nyɔat*. Other cattle can use pegs from any tree. *Puɔt* can be any (tree) *jiath*. There are usually two altars at home. One is in the middle of the *luak*, near or attached to one of the four poles of *gɛn* on the right side of the *luak*. This pole is called *thiriɛu*. It is the tallest pole supposed to reach the tip of the *luak*. The other altar is in the fireplace *wicgɔal* in the middle of the compound.

The altar *Riäk* must necessarily be out of *Nyɔat cordia rothii* tree. But why *Nyɔat* tree? *Nyɔat* is believed not to break how old it may be. It is not vulnerable to ants. But for man of Satan pajɔɔk he uses *thɔw* (another tree called balantines aegypium tree) as his altar *Riäk*. *Nyɔat* tree is sacred, so no evil acts are done with it. A person who died cọlwic mysteriously will have her or his altar erected on *Nyɔat*. Sometimes the *Nyɔat* suddenly grows in *cölwic* places or graves. When a green branch of *Nyɔat* is erected in *cölwic*'s place it grows. *Cölwic* altar is usually put in the field. When a cọlwic cattle is killed, its rope should be tied on the altar *Riäk* nyɔtä. This tree *Nyɔat* is never cut for any other purpose but its *fru*its are eaten. Should anyone wish to cut a shaft out of *Nyɔat*, he will have to tie bracelets on to the mother *Nyɔat* then chop off a piece as a shaft. The bracelet is supposedly its price. *Nuäär* believe that *Nyɔat* is God's sacred tree. The person *guan kakä*, on whose field the *Nyɔat* grew, should not prevent it. Actually, all altars are out of *Nyɔat* including the one usually carried to cattle camps. All the *Nyɔat* is not burnt for any other purpose. It does not wither normally like other plants.

During the spring when the cattle are no longer tethered in *luak* but outside, new food has come out (new harvest is already packed in jioŋ) beer is brewed, the altar at *thiriɛu* is brought out, pegged down and beer is poured and people (elders) including master of ceremonies pray to God that, "*Biɛl* God of this family, let the cattle sleep well, good health to the children, and fresh or pleasant living for all of us". Of course, all are sleeping outside, a symbol of new year. There is feasting and drinking of beer, oily food is put under the altar, sprinkle the beer into the *luak*, thök *luak*, *wicgɔal* and in front of the compound. This is the occasion when plenty of food is eaten. All the seated people are sprayed with beer.

Whenever a ritual or a sacrifice is being conducted, beer, milk, tobacco, and oil are thrown onto this altar and *thiriɛu*. When an old man quarrelled with one of his sons and throws tobacco on *thiriɛu* that child is assumed to die. Therefore, this altar is never removed nor taken out except in blessing the new harvest as indicated above or when people are migrating. When re-erecting it in a new byre, a small bull or ram has to be sacrificed or beer is brewed. In case there is no animal to offer for the moment, it is a pledge that something has to be killed in future. The altar at the fireplace outside *wicgɔal* is used for hanging on spears *Mut*i, and shields koti specially when there is no rain. Kuɔl is hung there for use during illness, or other things related to children. Two köli are usually hung in front of the byre from within and on the outside altar. Kuɔl is stored there because it dries up soon and *Nuäär* call it the cow of God. When there is no animal to be sacrificed, the kuɔl has to be used instead.

IV. *Dap ciek:* Birthing

The transition from being a couple to becoming a family with a child is a very important time in the relationship of the partners. We shall determine *Nuäär* attitude towards birth, prohibitions, precautionary steps, the place of birth and other implications.

Pregnancy and giving birth, according to the *Nuäär*, are the work of God no one has any say. Therefore, they are not celebrated as achievements.[85] However, when all the necessary prayers and rituals are completed and culminated in the woman giving birth, the marriage is thus stabilized.[86] The birth commences with the pregnancy of the mother. Traditionally, when a *Nuäär* woman becomes pregnant she does not tell her husband. She can, at most, talk of that her menstruation has not come. Sometimes the man's cousin could ask about the condition of the wife. He could be told that *nyiŋu liphɛ* she is expecting. This is not certain to be conception because her menstruation could break anytime. Real pregnancy could be confirmed after 3-4 months. The whole pregnancy is referred to in a symbolic manner *ciek ŋu ruetɛ or liphɛ* for early pregnancy. *Cɛ riɛm wäc* there is an alteration in the menstruation period by a month or two. Of course, *Nuäär* only rejoice in that the wife of so has produced or impregnated and nothing else of concern to them. It is not expressed in any form but inwardly appreciated because of what it reflects. It has revealed the couple's ability to procreate which is essential for the *Nuäär*.

For the *Nuäär*, any pregnancy outside of marriage is not taken as a disgrace. It is bad conduct from the children for not reading the feelings of their parents. Similarly, a bride's virginity and fidelity are not preconditions nor required to be proven. *Nuäär* have no way and, in fact; do not need to test the virginity of a girl. Moreover, it is not a prerequisite. Virginity is an unreasonable expectation because how could she avoid provoking the desire of a man as a teenager? Premarital sex exists but the girls/women who indulge do not talk about it because they would be considered promiscuous. All that matters is that the girl has no known fellows who coiter with her. There is no exclusive control or stern sexual morality. In fact, she is

---

85   Thomson Thɔan Tɛny interviewed on October 24, 2002 in Khartoum.
86   Oduyoye Kanyoro, op. cit., p.14.

expected to know how to make sex by observing others or practice in secret. A child born out of wedlock is acceptable. Marriages by consent are the acceptable pattern. Extra-marital relationships are common. It is normal to find an unmarried girl having children from more than one man. A girl made a woman with or without a child born is called *Kë-dap kɛl or dap rɛu.*

During pregnancy, women generally carry on with their usual work. It is, therefore, common for a woman to give birth while working in the fields. When she is in pain, she retires to the hut where she would be assisted by a mid-wife *gääm mään.*[87] The house where birthing takes place is a taboo or strictly forbidden to men and some women. A normal birth does not require special rituals. People only thank God for the good job done by the woman. But a complicated birth is sometimes attributed to adultery for which the woman in labour is encouraged to confess the illicit partner. Sacrifice may be made for her to safely deliver. For safe delivery and to protect herself and the child, a pregnant woman is instructed to observe certain taboos related to sexual relations and certain foods. The older women give her diet restrictions and instructions to attend to cultural structures. She is in a transitional period that is full of dangers or misfortunes. Some communities pray, bless and hail a child's birth. They plead to God to protect and safeguard the new child and grant good health and strength so that the baby may grow well.

The *Nuäär* see it more advisable that the bride delivers under her mother's care. However, due to difficulties, she could still deliver far away without problem. The essence of her mother is to make her know about delivery problems and to give advice. Besides, if she was playful, she could declare only to her parents, particularly the mother, the names of men who went with her. This may cause

---

87   A mid-wife is gääm *mään*. Gääm to *Nuäär* is somebody who waits to hold or catch something falling/pouring or leaking.

problems if known by her present husband. But if she confessed to parents, she will deliver normally and they can conceal her sexual dealings. Some women die at delivery because of no confession. If another man had impregnated her, *Nuäär* believe that the child would not come out until the actual father's name is mentioned. In case she does not, it is probable that the new-born will perish with its mother. When a woman with or without a child died while her marriage was not conducted (no *tuɔc* and no *ŋut- muɔt*), she is considered like a concubine or a girl impregnated but was compensated.

When a woman delivers, she has to be handled with care. Her placenta must be buried. Before it is done so the umbilical cord is cut twice. One cut into the stomach with blood and squeezed in until all the blood is finished. This being done then, it is tied twice again and cut leaving the two knots to the child. The placenta is very carefully handled because if done otherwise it will sever production and the woman becomes barren. It is carefully buried because it is taken as second twin. It must not be neglected nor just thrown away. If improperly buried, the woman shall cease to produce. It is therefore buried thus: It is hung on a *dura* straw cracked into two and then put into a hole with the supposed placenta head up and the hole is then covered with mud. Hence the placenta is well buried. The placenta is likened to a broken piece of human skull resulting from a stick hit. This piece or any broken bone has to be stored in a guord until this person (man) died (even several decades later) so as to bury it with the main body together. *Nuäär* believe that part of living body should not be buried.

The mid-wife who assists at the birth usually considers the child hers and sometimes she could give the name. When she goes home after delivering the baby, she may be offered *dura* in a *tuɔy*. She may see the newborn, time and again, and give advice to the mother to feed well and clean the baby often.

There are customs, which accompany the birth.[88] The mother must protect herself against evil spirits by observing such customs as not leaving her homestead and the child alone. During the baby's breastfeeding period, the husband should not have intercourse with her, lest a *thiaŋ* affects the child. Moreover, a new pregnancy may sap strength from the mother with her first child. A newly delivered woman comes out at 5 p.m. and is taken behind the house to urinate. Before returning in, she is made to step on the fire of a burning grass, prepared to cleanse her against footprints of hyena. If she has not been purified that way, the child is believed to cry throughout the night till morning. The mother of a dead infant should not enter houses with infants. It is assumed that she will carry the *phör*[89] and cause death to any child. She has to be purified accordingly. Whenever an infant died, its mother is cleansed with fiery grass within the house compound. This is conducted by old. The house is well plastered. The yeast flour is soaked in water and plastered or rubbed on the breasts of the woman. This is a disinfectant to dry the milk and suppress any possible inflammation of the breasts due to the milk. The old woman then tells her to, "Go among the other women". Any dish, guord, or spoon of that dead infant would be offered to the old woman who performed the purification. Whenever a man or woman whose home has a *phör* went to a home with *phör* infant, they have to be purified, before entering the home, to have their feet warmed with fire outside the compound and then proceed home. Otherwise, a home with *phör* is usually avoided. It is assumed that death is still looming in that house. All the women neighbours around have to be purified in that manner. Cleansing is

---

88   Ladislov Holy, Neighbours and Kinsmen, C. Hurst and company, Llondon 1974. p. 161
89   The disease killing the *phör* infant is called *phör*. It seems to be some impurity that can be contracted through interaction with such environment where the infant died. There is no physical association asserted.

applicable even to men who passed by the house. A woman who delivered or gave birth 2-3 months earlier is not affected.

The *Nuäär* believe that a woman, whose child died either in the stomach or upon delivery, is infected with *gɔal*.[90] When the ailment of the woman's body becomes severe, a cow, goat or ram has to be killed for this *gɔal*. Its meat is distributed among those attending the occasion. It is killed out of misfortune so its meat is not ritualised. All the relatives just hear that something has been killed for the *gɔal* of the wife of so. People then praise the act and pray that God give another one.[91]

But *thiaŋ* is different. A mother of an infant returning from a walk has to cleanse off *thiaŋ*. *Thiaŋ* infects even those infants with grown teeth. *Thiaŋ* is a disease that causes vomiting, dirhaea and broncopneumonia to infants. It is brought through sexual relations between a suckling wife (mother) and husband before weaning. Even contact with women and/or men in sexual practice can also cause it. To protect the infant against *thiaŋ* the parents slip a wristlet made of tiang's skin over the hand or the neck of the baby. Alternatively, an old lady would burn the feather of a he-cock and let the child smell the smoke. It is believed that the child will be cured. But if the child has been neglected until the dehydration stage, it will perish even if this process is performed. This is an unfortunate situation. But should the child survive and prosper, it now belongs to the whole community. The child's kinship bonds are established. Then the whole community becomes responsible for feeding the child and providing him or her with all the necessary things for balanced growth. This is according to the *Nuäär* concept of *gat ɛ gat nath dial* 'the child belongs to all the people'.

The excreta of the first-born are collected and put in the enclosure

---

90   *Gɔal* delivered with a dead child from the womb or instantly upon birth.
91   Dhil Gat*luak* Nyäk (died).

where its mother delivered. These should be taken out after one week. The mother has to take along a brush and put on her laps when she is squatting. Jien gatä The infant's first hair has to be shaved on the 8th day, a day after its remains are taken away. The hair is put in *rei* ker me tɔt a small guord and hung nhiam *duel* in front of the house from inside and only to be thrown away after the second born.

Birthing has initially an implication only for the woman and her husband. It has removed the ghostliness and revealed the man's ability to procreate. Apart from that, the birth of a child is hardly ever an occasion for joy except for the father and the mother. Birthing gives the mother a sense of accomplishment and inclusiveness. It is an announcement that the mystery has been accomplished. For the traditional *Nuäär* people, birthing is the accomplishment of divine mystery that cannot be expressed in rituals. Hence, birthing is not a big thing to *Nuäär* for which to summon or invite people in happiness. Only the parents of the newborn and their relatives know its goodness. The most interested person to note it, particularly a male child, is the gatuɔt head man because he is the one who registers and collects poll taxes. It is gatuɔt who follows the growth of this male child until reaching poll tax registration age after initiation.

The nuclear family continues to produce children. When a *Nuäär* says that somebody has children who have passed death, he means that they have recovered from the infant diseases- whooping cough, kilkil, juägh measles, yaws guɔl. At the age of 8 years, a child is said to have become a ran human being. Prior to that, *Nuäär* people do not rejoice because they are still not full human beings. Even then people pray to God to spare them to their parents.

The advocates of birth control believe that families should have only children they could afford to feed and care for decently. *Nuäär* do not believe in birth control because they are producing children to be shared with God. They are aware that few will die or be taken by God. So they continue to produce on the basis that, "We shall divide them with God".

In the *Nuäär* community, or most African communities for that matter, giving birth is significant. Through it, a new member is introduced to the community kuëciëŋ. The young mother becomes an honorable madam man gatä. This title ranks her as respectable woman of the clan worthy of consideration by the adult community. The term man gan 'mother of children' has other connotations. It means that she has a special status worth respect, consideration or reckoning with. She is not a rogue, prostitute, or barren. Henceforth, she would be addressed '*nya* ŋu' the daughter of (her father's name), or man ŋu the mother of (name of the newborn). Her maiden name drops. The father of the newborn is addressed gat ŋu son of so (his father's name) or guan ŋu father of (the new born). So *nya* ŋu, man ŋu, and gat ŋu, guan ŋu become the new titles with their associated status. But age-mates will address him by his bull or oxen-name. Both parents of the new baby acquire the status of parenthood, which enhances their privileges, and prestige in the community. Women who cannot have children for one reason or another are not accorded that respect and honour.

V. Identification - Naming: *Ciot.*

The senses of identity and of belonging begin and develop during childhood. These are derived from the meaning and significance mutually accorded by members of the family to the child and each other. There could be a child whose birth is accompanied by risks, which caused a later ailment of the mother. The parents may greatly value the child, as the embodiment of their own creative ability. A family may react in different ways to the death of a relative that occurred about the time of the birth of a child. The mother may have lost her brother at the time of her daughter's birth. Such was the grief. The family's history may have a period of distress. Perhaps this was due to the illness of the paternal grandmother, together with depression in the wife, all of which made the husband very anxious.

Names are symbols of identity. They identify the group one belongs or comes from. The baby acquires an individual, family, or group name. This name may reflect the history and origin of the group into which the child is born. The inherited clusters of geography and topography of the birthplace are made part of the newborn formally and ritually at birth. All these circumstances shape the individual's personality and his life.[92] Some individuals change names either to conceal inferior status or gain some comfortable anonymity so as to share identity with the dominant group. However, the meanings and connotations of names are known.

a. Factors that influence the naming of a child

Experiences or events that present many difficulties and threaten family stability are reckoned with and kept in memory as crises. The enormous range of situations and issues with which any family has to deal may be influenced from outside. They include the consequences of accidents, death and other factors outside the control of the family and its members. Internal catastrophies within the family or clan create individual and personal problems. These are all factors that influence the naming of a child.

The other physical elements also reckoned in naming are the place, the land and the soil the group is attached to historically and mythically. Some individuals continue to be identified with family birthplaces or distant ancestral homeland of several generations. Thus, all the features attached or attributed to people are reflected in naming.

---

92   Glazer and Moyniham, Harvard, 1975 pp. 31-52.

b. Child naming

Nuäär are not accustomed to celebrating birth or wedding anniversaries. But the place of birth, means of birth, natal care- even the moment of conception - are to some extent culturally reckoned with in naming children. Naming is some sort of identification from other persons in the family. A new child needs an identity and a social status to link him/her to his/her parents and others in society. We may distinguish between those that are mainly reflections of their relations to the environment (rup, wei, kay, bull, kir, yier, juat) and those that are reflections of their relations to one another in the social structure. Both refer to successions of events, which are of sufficient interest to the community for them to be noted and related to each other conceptually. The events they related are changes in the relationship of social groups. Both have limited and fixed notations. There are physical changes associated with rains and drought. *Nuäär* refer to some outstanding activity in process at the time of its occurrence.

A *Nuäär* name is carefully chosen, and its bestowal is connected with particular circumstances. The father may choose an ancestral name or of anybody, the family needs to be remembered in a loving manner. If a paternal or maternal grandparent dies while the mother is pregnant, the child will be named after him/ her.[93] The alternative is to give a name relevant to the situation.

Naming a child starts seven days after birth but is not a celebrated occasion. At this age it is called *phör*/ruɔr. Naming a child could be by a grandfather, mother or mother-in-law. The elders who prayed during this woman's marriage may give the name before the birth. For the successive births, the father gives the name. Other relatives, including friends, could name the child provided all have meanings. Ruɔr or *phör* is the same age but not grown teeth and therefore

---

93   Oduyoye Kanyoro, op. cit. p.47.

has no rights or entitlements when dead. But when its teeth have grown, it is considered a human being. The second brother shall marry a wife for him with the children called after the death. A baby from impregnated mother shall have its name during the prayers. If a misfortune happened or occurred to the father or child born after dead early brothers or sisters, this has to bear the name of the child.

Some Africans acquire new names at different stages in life or when they acquire new status in society. "It is even normal that for each new period of life, a new name is adopted which is one with the person. These are names that must always remain because they are "names from the internal".[94] There are other names linked to different situations of one's existence. The ancestral names internally continue the physical line of life and keep the departed relatives in personal immorality.[95] The mother gives the pet name she wishes to the child. The pet names have no mystical meaning but tell something about the bearers of the names. For example, if the birth occurs during rain, a girl child is named *nyanhial*, while a boy is *nhial*. The child may also be named after a significant social, religious, or political event happening at the time of his or her birth. In addition, individuals continue to acquire new names if they perform the remarkable and outstanding feat. The names have special significance in relation to their bearers.

A person's social identity develops in part from a name. A name often provides information on the sex and sometimes on the character of the individual. There are prefixes for boys' names and for girls' names. There are strict female and male names. Among the *Nuäär* a name could be identified from the prefix. For instance, males have *gat*, and ma annexed to the name. Girls are known with *nya* or *nyi*. There are names that identify twins, and their three

---

94   Oduyoye Ibid., p. 49.
95   John Mbiti, op. cit., p. 121.

successive brothers or sisters. So Both, (is the elder twin) Duoth, Bicok, and Bidit are male twins. Female twins are *Nya*-Both, *Nya*-Diet. If there are more twins, they would be offered any names of birds. The first child after twins is named Bol for both, and *Nya*-Bol. The second is Tot[96] or Gattot and *Nya*-Tot. The third is *Geŋ*, for both, and *Nya-Geŋ*. However, some other common or shared names for both genders also feature so much. Some of the shared names are: Jany, Kulaŋ, Kuɔny, Bol, Tot, *Geŋ* etc.

As for names like *Yay, Kai, Buɔm, Möy, Rɛl, Yuit, Luit, Mäi, Pɛt,* they are associated with either the structure of the newborn or the circumstances of pregnancy and birth. They are male names while an addition of *nya* before each makes it female. *Kai, Buɔm,* and *Möy* are male children conceived without menstruation. This is abnormal to *Nuäär*. Such children are to be born in front of the home compound. They are associated with abnormal power that enabled their conception, unlike others. They are treated differently lest they affect either of their parents and grandparents. Yuit and Luit are the same- meaning tiny. But Mäi and Pɛt are dry season- February. This must be when they were born.

Altar, windscreen and shrines of the household are targets in rituals. *Riäk* or *Buɔr* must have been born either under the *Riäk/Buɔr* or on the occasion of their erection.

Spear names are peculiar to definite families. For instance, *Mut, Mun, Tuac, Wud, Lɔny, Nyang, Guɔr, Bidh, Puɔt, Taŋ, Chur, Yiɛw, Thɔl, Muɔl, Waŋmac, Ber, Waŋ, Koc,* etc. are specific names. This is identity naming.

For a boy or a girl whose father died either during his/her birth, or while in conception is called *Gai (Nya-Gai)*. The idea is that this woman will be helpless or suffer/poor that she lost her husband. Other names associated with death or helplessness after death are *Ruɔt, Liay, Biliu, Kuɔny, Mun, Madir, Dirpiny, Mɔlpiny,* etc. The

---

96 Which could be for both male and female.

name of a child after man's slaughter is *Thoŋ*. This name is given by those who were killed. But the family of the slain name the child born for the dead or slained through ghost marriage *Ter* meaning feud. This is supposed to remind the newborn later that there is a feud with such a family.

There are the names of the instruments and articles of prayers or invocations. Lam is the invocation or prayer while *phi, cak, juac, tab, puɔgh, ŋëth* etc are used to manage it.

Names of colours are mostly of bulls slaughtered during marriage - wedding ceremony or conception of the mother of the new infant. So Mabor, (my name) means white, Macar is black, Malual is red, but Ma*nya*ng, Maker, and Marial are spotted colours. The actual colours are without the Ma. To convert them to female name is to prefix *Nya* before the colour such as *Nya*borä, *Nya*car, *Nya*lual, *Nyanyaŋ*, *Nya*kera, *Nya*rial etc. Giving the meaning of those names in English would make, Mabor Mr. White, Macar Mr. Black, Malual Mr. Red and vice versa for females.

The parents, grandparents and other members of the family circle are preoccupied with searching for a name as the identity of the child. It will serve to remind the group of its basic original identity, its roots and the circumstances of duress the family had to undergo while in the process of begetting this child. The child grows up in the family, sometimes with brothers and sisters. He is made aware of himself and of his position in the family group. He also lives in other environments that have an impact on their life. When he grows mature and marries, he will follow this pattern of naming children to reflect an event, occasion, catastrophe, historical reckoning etc.

So, naming in general has to do with the whole life experienced by the family including the hardships, ailments and circumstances that prevailed during conception and birth. The name of the first child from a wife married in the *Nuäär* conventional way is usually determined at the wedding ceremony prayers. For the rest of the children, any relative could give a name with connotation for the family.

VI. Divorce or dissolution/termination of the marriage covenant

Nuäär have neither laws nor procedures for divorce because their society attaches high importance to the continuation of marriage. The union created by marriage should be held to last even beyond death. A couple may separate and so cease to play the roles of husband and wife. Divorce or separation in *Nuäär* society is a social disruption in the family. It is complicated by (a) the status of small children i.e. which parent will have custody and bring them up and (b) the bride-wealth. Sometimes divorce entails the return of marriage payment. But to *Nuäär* the bride-wealth is the guarantee of the stability of marriage. It irrevocably fixes the status of a woman's children As an incentive to the woman folk who received it, there is an apparent difficulty in returning it.

There is no defined divorce apart from the circumstances regarding bars to marriage indicated in chapter one 6 under other social factors for family integrity- (a) divorce *dagh* (b) adultery *dhom* (c) attempted suicide *ŋaph* (d) gossip *löm* (e) thievery *kual*. The issue of impotent and a contagious disease are bars to marriage too. There must be circumstances or typical arguments that the society holds to justify a wife in leaving her husband or a husband in driving away from his wife i.e. when a man can separate with his wife. In rare circumstances, a man can divorce if (i) his wife is repeatedly unfaithful, repeatedly disobedient and quarrelsome (with co-wife).

However, those issues are usually subjected to consultations with relatives to ascertain if such grievances would allow for the release of the woman.

Divorce is not too frequent because marriage and procedures and rituals as well as peoples' comments on couples' behaviour generally make it clear that lasting unions are valued. This is clearly indicated in the advices and safeguards to the newlywed couples covered in chapter three-item I (h) –(ii).

This ideal *Nuäär* marriage faced drastic influences that socially changed several aspects of it. The extent of those social changes is overviewed in the next chapter.

CHAPTER FIVE
Social Change in the *Nuäär* Marriage

The discovery and exploitation of the oil engaged Nuäär as paid labour force- thus introduced them to money economy. The north-south intractable war had massively displaced people internally within the country and to the neighbouring countries and the northern Sudan. This displacement and settlement in the host societies have resulted in changes in Nuäär attitudes and perceptions. All the above have had profound impact on the Nuäär traditional ways. The Nuäär ideal marriage narrated above is one such aspect that has undergone drastic changes due to other internal and external factors. The 1980s second civil war depleted the cattle resource and bred gun-wielding military youth who had no regard for the elder generations; displacement; spread of Christian gospel; and migration. These have affected, in a remarkable way, the *Nuäär* bride-wealth, preparation for marriage and rituals, the purpose of marital unions and the termination of the marriage covenant. It shall be found that the *Nuäär* marriage is inflated in bride-wealth because of hardships in the upbringing of the girls being married. Many marriage procedures are skipped. Marriage with money has been imposed by the hardships and uncertainty of any available livestock- cattle and goats, back home. The proxy marriages are common particularly for the migrants or *Nuäär* in diaspora. The culture of the host society of displacement had encroached and inserted some of its practices. Above all, Christianity has altered certain cattle rights and among some families the Bible is now entitled to a cow. These are a result of war.

I. War

The impact of war has been enormous. It has deprived human beings of their dignity, left thousands of orphans, and families deprived of their breadwinners. Life-sustaining activities are lacking generally. It has caused massive displacement and forced many to flee to the other towns in the country in search of safety, food and treatment. Gone are their homes, some of their loved ones, their precious properties, their herds and other means of survival. Above all many have been forced into the liberation army where many lost their lives as a result of inter-factional fighting. This, in turn, rendered many as ghosts with several hundred women widows. Part of the movement of citizens has been a result of widowhood and rape even of legal wives.

War had its own consequences on marriage priority and bride-wealth determination. The war has put the whole *Nuäär*land in turmoil. First and foremost, the generation gap and respect have been eroded. Looting and harassment of elders were common unabated practices. Even a part of the home could be cleared of utensils and edible things. Any inquiry from the head of the household was considered an undue interference which at least deserved punishment. Without doubt *Nuäär* take this act a total breakdown of norms of respect and privacy of the female sector within the home. Gone with this respect was the usual fear for a would-be in-law that was the practical attitude towards everybody.

Nuäär attitude was regulated by fear that one day, by intent or mistake; they could be in-laws through the marriage of their children. The young men dragged into the liberation war did tamper with the mothers' utensils and (food store) *nak*. This is not allowed by *Nuäär* culture. This generation is fined with one cow for such misconduct and disrespect for the mothers' confidential store.

War brought gun as a source of power for the protection of the household. If one or few sons from a family enlisted with the liberation army of Southern Sudan, they would have priority in marriage thus upsetting the family marriage list. Furthermore, if any of their sisters got married, the guns they hold are entitled to a cattle right in the bride-wealth. These guns are claimed to have protected the girl, being married, from abduction. So, the war introduced the gun into the bride-wealth entitlements.

The war further made looting and abduction a common way of acquiring cattle and wives. Some girls are raped and abducted at gun point. It may happen that from one family a girl was raped and cattle were also looted. Whenever the girl's father got an opportunity to ask for bride-wealth, he would be given from the looted cattle. He may be lucky to have back his own looted cattle for his daughter's marriage. Hence, by rotation, his own cattle were used to marry his daughter. This is another impact of the war. Therefore, the authorisation to marry is in the groom's hands. He decides to marry by abducting or raping a girl and pays for her from looted cattle. The bride-wealth is not negotiated; the groom instead determines how many he can offer. This violated the conventional steps, *käm tuac*, lär *kuen*, *luɔm*, *cuɛc*, *tuɔc*, *buɔr*, *muɔt* etc. Practically all the steps have been skipped or relegated. He may only exercise the *buɔr* whenever he eloped with the girl from the neighbourhood and sought to handle the marriage formally with her parents. The war has facilitated all this mess. The total reversal of the procedures has effectively undermined the scrutiny for relations and other bars to marriage. In retaliation, girls ran away from rape and abduction but ended as displaced in the other parts of the country. Other young men escape conscription and go to the various towns in Northern Sudan as persons displaced by the war. All these youngsters get lumped up in urban centres without alternative programmes. Some resorted to domestic work; others went to building construction, with a few loitering in the towns selling cigarettes, second-hand clothes, and school textbooks without licenses. The girls and boys encounter in the church compounds, wedding dances, and other cultural occasions. They develop an interest in themselves and venture to marry without regard for parental consent or involvement. The easiest available alternative action is to elope and happen what may. When their elders intervene, they may find the young people too young to marry or may be related in one way or another. Moreover, certain social factors may not allow them to marry. Whatever is the case, some damage has been done to both families.

Another factor had been the impregnation that has become too common. It was rare among the *Nuäär* to impregnate a girl because it was not easy to induce her to sexual intercourse. As a consequence of war, many ladies are widowed, raped and abandoned, or impregnated. Any unions as a result are not considered normal legal marriages. Therefore, with impregnation, there is no force to marriage except the payment of damages. In addition to those things above, displacement has an impact on the *Nuäär* marriage and culture in general.

II. Displacement

Displacement has been the result of the erratic eruption of fighting between the Sudan government forces and the liberation fighters. These people have been forced into destitution only rescued by the humanitarian assistance from the Non-Govermental Organizations (NGOs). This displacement has placed these people under different stresses. This new class of homeless people became self-settled in the outskirts of major towns in the North in search of safety, food and treatment. Due to the recent South Sudan internal conflict thousands of people, including the *Nuäär*, are settled in Protection of Civilian camps by the United Nations Mission in South Sudan (UNMiSS). This precarious life in those camps has its own culture. It has made hardship on the *Nuäär* people with great impact on the scrutiny of a spouse, relations, and bride-wealth inflation due to initiated meetings with sisters, mothers, and fathers-in-law all of which demand financial payment.

It was important that the woman being married belonged to the family. This involved the parental consensus on the girl to be married for the purpose. Hence, mutual attraction of the young couple was not the determining factor for marriage. With displacement, the young people select and arbitrarily decide to marry there and then. They would, at times, run away to by-pass and undercut their elders' role. This role may be viewed as a tedious and time-wasting process. So, these youth marry alone and adopt the style of walking hand in hand. It was earlier mentioned that procreation, not companionship, was the main objective of marriage. *Nuäär* women do not walk hand in hand, in companionship, with their husbands. They walk together when fetching food elsewhere or migrating. Otherwise, they do not walk together in companionship. Occasionally they walk but the man leads followed by the woman. *Nuäär* believe that the woman accepts this following and pleads to God for the man to proceed to die first and she remains to inherit the household. Because the youth in displaced camps/towns marry out of love, not a deep one even, they share no one in the choice of the partner. There was no scrutiny about both spouses regarding relations and/

or other bars to marriage. It may only be discovered later that both may have issues that would not permit their marriage. But because of love, they may resist breaking their marriage and so decide to keep away from their parents. When life becomes hard for them, they may divorce there and then. The girl becomes *kë* and the young man a divorcee. This is a scar that shall keep haunting them. They become divorcees of each other. The reasons for their divorce shall henceforth concern whoever wished to make any of them a partner.

Wherever it was possible to present for marriage, another obstacle was that the family marriage councils were not to be found in the areas of displacement. Hence, marriages are settled by young relatives who may be unknowledgeable about cattle rights' entitlements. Based on their situation they may opt or prefer money to use for the enjoyment of life or their education. The bride-wealth may be thirty to fifty million pounds, being the monetary value of more than one hundred cows. This is above the ideal cattle rights of twenty six to thirty-eight cows. Usually, the elders at home would not recognise such deals. Consequently, the marriage may break up. Even the groom's parents and other relatives may not bless but rather detach themselves from such a marriage. So in the event of no scrutiny, people severed by customs not to marry do so in disregard. Young men out of love and without any financial ability decide to run away with girls. These unions are usually broken because there is nothing to offer to the bride's people. Nobody would bother if the man lacked the means to maintain himself and his wife. This is usually considered his concern and shame that he will share with nobody except his immediate relatives or parents.

In a marriage normally conducted and handled by elders within the displaced camps/towns, inflation in bride-wealth has been realised. There is a cash equivalent of bride-wealth. This payment, though exorbitant, has the same consequences of marriage. Among the issues forced into cattle negotiations are the sufferings the parents have been experiencing under displacement. Sharia law is very severe in Khartoum against brewing alcohol. But displaced women resorted to local beer-making although those with the purchasing power may not be the displaced themselves. This activity has exposed the families, even visitors to the displaced, to jail sentences and fines, if the 'public order police' got hold of them. The atalla used for digging the beer into the underground cover is rewarded with cattle right as the source that helped bring up the girl in question. Moreover, the imprisonment of the bride's mother has to be compensated due to the suffering the mother severely endured.

Another development in the then Ler province (now a county in the current Unity State) was that the stepmother of the bride would be considered for a cow as right in the marriage. The intension being to soften the conspiracies or envies of co-wives wuɔckɛ nyagh.[97] It is believed that the stepmother would henceforth respect the groom and also take the stepdaughter as hers. She would have no reason to discriminate the bride since she got a right there.

The mother of the bride has a cow for her friend- preferably a female one. She is thus encouraged to have friends as is common with the fathers. It must be noted that this right is usually reciprocated.

New additions are talking to the girls, mothers-in-law and fathers in-law all of whom demanded financial payment. Issues like dumb, blind and deaf girls to be tipped with money to be able to converse with the brothers and companions of the groom, are raised during the youth's first meeting. It has become a practice for young people to meet and converse. This involves payment of money otherwise conversation would not take place. The supposed dumb, blind, and deaf girls would continue to behave so until

---

97 Peter Ɖuɛn Köl, interviewed on May 31, 2004 in Khartoum.

money has been paid to lure them to speak. The young men cannot go around this trap because those very girls are their spokespersons. They are complicating factors who must be pleased to make the other marriage procedures at home go smoothly. Similarly, the groom with a few of his friends should meet the (mothers-in-law) *manthuyni*. This is in line with the conventional *Nuäär* procedure before the *muɔt nyal*. So whatever is offered to *manthuyni* is a mere gift. The fathers-in-law are to be visited also. These three categories deserve money payment beyond the bride-wealth.

Through displacement, the *Nuäär*, alongside others, have been exposed to influences from the host society. The cultural influence of the host society in displacement has made a hybrid of *Nuäär* culture. Sheila- the dresses and food items to take to the bride's parents is encroaching as a borrowed custom. Hena- the black decoration of the hands and legs is finding its way through the *Nuäär* as bride make-up with the women companions. Lunches are organised with the expected payment of money. Documented invitations to friends and relatives for marriage weddings and parties are practices entering very fast into the community. It involves payment for printing that is not part of the marriage but extraordinary expenses. The present youth understand and dance the African/western music better than *Nuäär* cultural dances.

III. Migration- Nuäär in diaspora and the monetisation or dollarization of marriage

Nuäär in diaspora encourage marriage by proxy. Choice of a spouse and negotiations are made by the relatives, but wealth is paid by the groom.

Migration has clearly played an important part in providing households and parents back home with much-needed income. Some of them send money to parents/relatives to meet an array of needs including foodstuffs, medical treatment, education, clothing and travel expenses. However, the form and frequency of payments are only known to individual families. It is only apparent that the money received is carefully controlled to fill the vacuum left by the migrants. Male migration has a profound impact on household subsistence. But as migrants ferry funds back to their relatives, their migration or labour, for that matter, is strategically located.

The *Nuäär* people in the diaspora should be deviant because they have supposedly become a part of the sub-culture. In adapting to the different social circumstances, they should have formed different values, beliefs, and patterns of behaviour. But that they are giving full prerogative to their parents and relatives to choose wives and they pay for all the arrangements- engagement, wedding and issue of license or marriage certificate from the church or court, travel documents and tickets, makes these marriages ideal. A possible explanation was given[98] that they discovered, in comparison, that certain *Nuäär* cultural values and family relations deserve to be maintained. So, once a native lady is married, language and identity do not pose any problem.

Others[99] see that back at home *Nuäär* society has defined and designated functions with specific confines and rights. The *Nuäär* woman is subordinate to the man. This may not be there in a foreign culture where the marriage may be a mutual understanding between the spouses in disregard of parental consent. *Nuäär* are also sensitive to and obsessed with hen-peg. A *Nuäär* man must be seen fully controlling his home without rival or restricted authority.

98　According to Mr. Daniel Nen *Nhial*- a Southern Sudanese *Nuäär* who migrated to USA, where he acquired citizenship, but dared not cut the cultural links with the original home. He came home to marry and I had the opportunity to attend his marriage and then interviewed him on January 9, 2004.

99　Like Thomas Wicjial Chɔap- a Juba University student, an observant of this attitude towards marriage.

Since marriage is a family relation between parents and relatives of the respective spouse, any problems that ensue usually concern the two families. Bride-wealth would be secured in the hands of in-laws and can be obtained upon divorce. Foreign marriages are therefore discouraged because of the difficulty in getting the wealth back due to distances and other matters. To return cattle is a punishment for the girl's parents for the bad conduct of their daughter.

This marriage by proxy is much more beneficial to the relatives because all the expenses are born by the groom. The whole process is monetised. Though the migration has monetised the *Nuäär* marriage, on the other hand, it encouraged and relied much on family choice. Because *ciek ɛ ciek cieŋ* the woman is of the household, the groom would rely very much on the parental approval of a girl. Marriage by proxy emphasises the family decision and full participation. The groom would be of some role if he had prior knowledge about the girl otherwise it is both families who decide. The bride may not have seen the would-be husband but would rely on the approval of her parents. Moreover, being married and taken to a foreign land is a great development for an individual girl. It is linked to the first world which means good life too. Most youths are adventurous and opt to migrate to find fortunes in life. They are entitled to a good and decent life. There are situations where the youth (boy and girl) find themselves abroad and decide to marry but wait for their respective parents to work out the conventions. They stay apart until there is a response to unite and celebrate their marriage in a church where they are. The marriage discussions and formal rituals and celebrations are videotaped and sent to them to verify the witnesses and the attendants. So marriage by proxy is recommended by each of the couples and should be *duely* looked into. However, certain complications do occur where the couple might be thousands of kilometres apart- across the continent, and only work things by correspondence. They may not know much about how each handled herself/himself. This may result in breaking the marriage. The parents at home have to keep up with the disappointment.

Of a striking concern is why the *Nuäär* migrants do not fully absorb into the host societies and marry from there since they are assumed to have integrated into that life. It has been said that love is so blind that it sees no caste, religion or culture. That these migrant *Nuäär* opt for girls sent by relatives from back home is of interest. It may be worth looking into. Could it be that they intend to come back when the home situation improved? Or the life with foreign ladies is hard to go along with? Perhaps they feel that the basic values of *Nuäär* life should not be lost. Hence **Nuäär** in diaspora monetised the marriage and for that matter, the dollar marriage is very expensive. It equally inflated the rate for the domestic suitors. They also strengthened the family choice of a partner- the *Nuäär* concept of *ciek ε ciek cieŋ*. Therefore, the *Nuäär* group in diaspora may manage to sustain some of their cultural values handed through the generations. While embracing or integrating into the western culture, they have to continue to speak and promote the teaching of their language to the children.

IV. Christian Gospel

The *Nuäär* who are christened, tend to give up certain cattle bride rights associated with spirits and other beliefs. But they maintained the other entitlements and added that the church be given a cow for the Bible instead of the spirits. Moreover, the church ceremonies are another development in addition to the traditional procedures. There are marriages transferred to the church for consummation and blessing.

Modifications in *Nuäär* marriage ceremonies include the provision of a wedding gown, engagement ring, marriage photograph and the dancing party soon after that. The normal advices from parents to the girl have nothing to do with such modified marriages. The groom is not told anything about the girl. What is done in the church involves the vows and promises to be one and rely on one another until death separated them. The blessing and prayers involve that the couple should live in peace and be blessed with children that would reflect the will of God. Honeymoon holidays are adoptions which are optional. However, it is common for newlyweds to spend at least one week in one of the hotels in the town. In the traditional *Nuäär* marriage, there is nothing as a special month for the couples to be alone. Once the handing and taking over processes have been completed, the community recognizes the groom and the bride as a family. They are private to themselves and no one would mind thereafter.

All these factors have severed the *Nuäär* marriage conventions. They have deprived it (marriage) of the traditional rituals and ceremonies to gather the people and the household spirits to witness, enjoy and pray to God to bless the couple with children and good health. No longer are both households able to advice and/ or follow up the welfare of their children- the couple. This has consequently eased break down of marriages. Despite those many penetrations into the *Nuäär* traditional marriage, the *Nuäär* still cling to their traditional ideas of what a marriage should be. They also insist on how marriage should be made legal after many aspects of their life have been profoundly changed.

Summary and Conclusion

We sum up what has been done so far and underline the most important stages, events and rituals. The issues to highlight are the decision to marry, the actual marriage itself, rituals and the birth, and naming of children. The collectivity of *Nuäär* marriage is reflected in the various stages. *Buɔr* and *muɔt nyal* have great impact even on the children marriages and rituals' performances.

a. Summary

The *Nuäär* marriage is associated with their belief that life is the continuation of the family genealogical tree and that one's name is perpetuated. Hence, to marry or be married is a right no *Nuäär* should ever be deprived of. Even the disabled are entitled to marriage and children. Accordingly, families, clans or households have an obligation, at least, to procure one wife for a male and ensure that their daughter is married in any case. Marriage is therefore a collective responsibility of the family. Relatives are involved in the cattle payment, spouse scrutiny and acceptance, and celebrations or ceremonies. By kinship extension, marriage is restricted for people inside the ego, totem, and/or age-set. Even relatives on both paternal and maternal sides up to six generations are prohibited from marrying. Sexual behavior is generally regulated with or without marriage. This is to safeguard against incest or marrying from those taboo-associated people.

Because marriage is a right and necessarily outside one's clan, *Nuäär* practice starts with monogamy, exogamy, polygamy, polygyny and a corrupted form or their own model of polyandry. Marriage among the *Nuäär* is eternal life. So they prefer that a wife be obtained by negotiations and the payment of bride-wealth.

Marriage among the *Nuäär* is prioritized according to age and household seniority. The list is to be adhered to under normal circumstances. Each member in the list is usually contributed herds for his first marriage which is considered the wife of the family. Successive wives are his own choice and bride-wealth is borne by him with his friends although the female offspring are then enjoyed by all the family upon their marriage. The first family wife entails family choice and consent to the marriage; and their collective responsibility for payment of the bride-wealth. All the family, relatives and spirits, participate directly and indirectly in the arrangement and consummation of this marriage.

Marriage is a key moment that follows a few years after initiation. Both the initiation and the marriage are events that serve to break the bonds of the individual with childhood and the unmarried state. We found this when the male child moved to the byre of young men and elders to take up responsibilities related to and relevant with the *luak*. By the age of nine, he is put in charge of herding the calves, sheep and goats alone or in company with other boys of his age. A boy of ten years herds cattle with his older brothers up to a distance of five miles in a day. The girls, meanwhile, learn the women's work; cooking, carrying water, chopping and collecting wood, milking livestock and weeding gardens during the season.

In those days by the age of twenty to twenty-five years, the wildness and carefree days of the youth were now getting over. The youth should seek for a wife to marry. He should get married and have children. It should be realised that the young man's transition starts with *kuud*, guan*tuai*, *kuen*, pai*muɔt* and finally becomes respected as cɔw*nyal*- husband of the daughter. He gently grows old and is therefore expected to display wisdom and become a respected member of the tribe. The children produced start the life cycle again in the same sequence.

The individual makes a family and thus gets re-integrated into the adult community. But *Nuäär* differentiates between family-making and marriage. The ideal marriage is that of *nyadhuɔri* a fresh girl or virgin in the narrow sense. But concubinage and levirate or sororate are methods of making a family. Disregarding how many children were born under these last situations, *Nuäär* consider the relationship as friendship and not marriage in their conventional terms. Marriage outside the kin is the appropriate one for the *Nuäär*. Bride-wealth entitlement, incest and other taboos prohibit marriage otherwise.

We tried to cover the *Nuäär* marriage in chronological order and examined how the couple meets, and the reaction of their respective families, friends and the community. From there we discerned the decision to marry and the associated decisions such as *luɔm*, *cuɛc*, *buɔr*, *tuɔc*, *muɔt*. The decision to marry depends on the influence of parents and expedience.

Hence, paph yiɣni, *cuɛc*, *tuɔc* and *buɔr* are by family decision. But *luɔm* involves mostly the taking, to the bride's home, of engagement or booking cattle earmarked for the *luak*. It is soon followed by paph yiɣni an exploratory meeting between both elders. This sort of background investigation takes place even though the possible spouses considered appear to have no trouble on the surface. Both elders check into every detail of the person's lineage and life. If they are discovered to be related to someone in that family by blood, the proposed marriage is deemed impossible. *Cuɛc* is the second driving of cattle mostly those to go to the *yɔk dɔaŋni* grand parents. At times they are brought and possibly delivered to rightful owners. During *tuɔc* and *buɔr* the rest of cattle are completed. While marriage negotiations are underway, the father of the bride will insist that each of his close relatives be given livestock. The marriage becomes legal when the bride's relatives are paid the cattle they demanded. But should the couple disappoint the elders by eloping, the marriage shall be conducted in an atmosphere of recklessness and disobedience. The groom must meet these demands for bride-wealth but also try to hold a few cattle to support his bride. It is worth noting that he, earlier on, made several rounds of visits to the relatives trying to get contributions for his bridal herd. So, when there is remarkable progress in those discussions, the groom will come to the bride's home, the centre for discussion, driving a few of the remaining cattle rights. These could include gifts from his friend *määdh*. The gifts may go to the friend of the bride's father. The *määdh* can also offer the *yaŋ* cow of their mother-in-law *manthuydiɛn*. During this event, the groom arrives at the bride's homestead wearing a handsome civet cat skin draped over his waist. Sometimes he decorates himself with ashes of cow dung and wears feathers, necklaces and nice underwear covered by the skin. Usually, that will be considered an ample dress for such occasion.

After the cattle negotiations are enacted, including the pledges finally agreed upon, the groom should arrange to take the bride to his homestead. We then proceeded to the wedding and the establishment of a married life. The rituals and prayers conducted there are to install her in the household compound. She owns that house, until they move out with her husband to a new abode, if none was prepared for her earlier.

According to the *Nuäär* marriage conventions, *buɔr* and *muɔt* are very, if not the most, important steps. If a woman's *buɔr* was not conducted, it will affect the marriage of her daughter. Her *buɔr* and *muɔt* must be conducted simultaneously after which her daughter's marriage can be handled. *Nuäär* believe that such a woman was not incorporated into the rights of that family and so her daughter cannot be put to such rights before her.

The most usual marriage procedure starts with a formal betrothal, preceded by negotiations of some kind between the partners or their guardians, and followed by a formal public inauguration of the union. The evasion of formal rules of marriage negotiations can be done by girls who do not like their fathers' choice and/or boys who cannot afford to raise their bride-wealth cattle. Elopement is another way of circumventing parental choice and forcing the consent of elders to a marriage agreed on by a young couple. Parents would, therefore, have no objection to a suitor who has already approached their daughter. Apart from that, it is not possible to get married without any formalities. Whether people cannot afford or do not attach importance to them, there is no permitted alternative to those marriage formalities.

In the context of time and the people involved, *Nuäär* marriage is an order of events of outstanding significance. Most of the wedding feasts or celebrations take place in the bride's village except for *muɔt nyal* and her that cooking which necessarily has to take place at the groom's. All the men, kin and friends from the groom's village attend it and are entertained with food and beer. The wed-dings and other ceremonies are occasions of vows, invocations, social feasts, and bride-wealth payment. The normal marriage is consummated in the thirteenth stage of the wedding. This stage usually takes place, preferably after the harvest, when there is enough food for the ceremonial feasts. Of course, the *Nuäär* have no honeymoon but the bride (woman) is called *Kaw* till she produced a child. In the meantime, she is encouraged to practice the new roles by joining other couples in social groups' ceremonies.

A domestic event that is supposed to greatly change the circumstances in which a family lives is the birth of a child. Each child is the prime responsibility of the parents. When a child reaches that stage of development where his independence and personal identity begin to unfold, the cycle of *Nuäär* life starts to roll. But *Nuäär* do not celebrate the birth of a child nor the naming. They are considered a divine work in which no one has a role. Hence they are not achievements to rejoice over.

b. Conclusion

It can be concluded that *Nuäär* marriage is guided by two concepts related to eternity and the commonality of life. The belief that life is eternal entitles a *Nuäär* the right to marry and be married at least once. Marriage means the reproduction of offspring to perpetuate life. To *Nuäär* no living person should be allowed to *riau* wither away or annihilate. S/he should be helped by all means available to have children to continue the family tree. This is a right that the entire family is obliged to meet. The second precept is that *ciek ɛ ciek cieŋ* the woman is the wife of the household. This woman becomes the property of the household and is to be incorporated into that family totem, rituals, and ceremonies. As the lady of the house *ciek cieŋ*, she is first and foremost involved in running the home and bearing children. She is not yet but expected to produce offspring as a source of labour and also perpetuate the family through their marriages and thus enlarge relationship. She assumes her status and the associated rights in that family. As part and parcel of the household, they have the right in her choice, marriage and cattle payment. All the stages being followed are to ensure that the family makes a consensual choice and the woman is duly incorporated into the home of her husband. Whatever variations or deviations exist they never blur the above two facts. They reflect, as well as confirm, the collectivity of *Nuäär* marriage. Their realization means the implementation of the *Nuäär* culture.

The collectivity of *Nuäär* marriage is reflected in that courtship is regulated and marriage required parental consent and is often arranged. A young man is allowed to find a girl. He proposes her for his parents to approve or disapprove his choice. Should they reject his choice, he starts to look again. If they agree, then the marriage procedure begins. He takes some cattle to her home as an engagement token *luɔm* to show his commitment. It also shows that the girl has agreed to be married. Many men began their marriages by first engaging *yɔk liphä* young girls below the age of puberty. Marriage is conducted outside one's cultural kin group. *Nuäär* are bound by incest, bride-wealth cattle entitlements, and the concept that the female or woman belongs to nowhere or everywhere outside the circle.

The issue of a guided spouse choice raises the question of whether *Nuäär* women ever marry the men they love. In the *Nuäär* society, a man marries a woman; a woman never marries a man. *Nuäär* girls have no choice of who to marry but bring potential husbands or suitors for scrutiny and choice by the parents. It is the family to decide because marriage is creation of relationships involving the family and the clan, for that matter. So individuals have minimum effect or role in this family affair.

The *Nuäär* marriage may appear as fragile due to the impact of the factors enumerated in chapter five above. Those factors have disturbed the *Nuäär* as individuals, families and a tribe struggling to preserve their identity and culture. Nevertheless, the *Nuäär* people still consider marriage as a sacred institution. It is still relevant and conveniently arranged to impress every aspect of *Nuäär* life. The nuclear family created through marriage is, at first, an interdependent socio-economic unit that gradually extends to the wider kinship network.

Though the factors - war, displacement, migration and the Christian gospel, illustrated above had affected *Nuäär* life, rules and customs, many *Nuäär* people still cling to their traditional ideas of what a legal marriage should be. Those displaced and in diaspora still continue to marry with the cash equivalent of a fraction of the cattle bride-wealth. A man who earns his bride-wealth could easily assert his independence in approaching his marriage i.e. deciding the girl he must marry. But some of the *Nuäär* gentlemen in diaspora did not dare to cut loose relations with the kin at home country. They instead shared and subordinated their freedom of choice in marriage to the older generation back home.

The constraints focused in Chapter Four VI do not make the marriage to lapse. It is therefore hoped that, through detailed elaboration of the marriage practices, much of the *Nuäär* culture has been exposed.

Appendix 1
Ideal Nuäär Bridewealth

(1) yaŋ yiɣni (1) cow for the bride's master of ceremonies, the opener of marriage discussions, pledged during in-laws joint council meeting.

(2) waay (2) cow for the paternal aunt;
(3) yaŋ guan nyal (3) cow of bride's father;
(4) yaŋ man nyal (4) bride's mother's cow;
(5) yaŋ kuɔdh guan nyal (5) the cow for the bride's father's spirit;
(6) yaŋ kuɔdh mandɛ (6) the cow for the bride's mother's spirit;
(7) yaŋ guandɔŋ (7) grand father's cow;
(8) yaŋ mandɔŋ (8) grandmother's cow;
(9) yaŋ guanlen (9) cow for the paternal uncle;
(10) yaŋ billä (10) *Biel* God's cow;
(11) yaŋ manlen (11) maternal aunt's cow;
(12+13) daw + ruath dɔŋä guanleenä (12+13) calf + small bull of grand paternal uncle;

(14+15)daw+ruath dɔŋä näärä wutä
(16)yaŋ guandɔŋ pek närä
(17)yaŋ jɔak pukä
(18) yaŋ mandɔŋ pek närä

(19+20) yaŋ näärä + thäkdɛ

(21+22)daw + ruath dɔŋä näärä-mandɛ

(23+24) daw + ruath guanleenä

(25) thäk guandɛ
(26) thäk guanleenä

(14+15) calf + ruath grand parent's man's uncles;
(16) grand father maternal uncle;
(17) cow for behind the ashes;
(18) grandmother maternal uncle;
(19 + 20) maternal uncle + his bull;
(21+22) calf +small bull of grandmother- maternal uncles;
(23 +24) calf + ruath of paternal uncle;
(25) father's bull;
(26) bull of paternal uncle.

Appendix 2A
Nuäär Marriage
Short Form of Settlement No. 1
(Kuen Nuäärä min ciekdien)

	Total.
I. <u>Pek Guandɛ- Father's side.</u>	
1. Yaŋ guandɛ, kuɔdhdɛ (cow of father and of the God/spirit)	2
2. Yaŋ mandɛ, kuɔdhdɛ (cow of mother and of her God/spirit)	2
3. Yaŋ Jɔak Pukä (Cow of the spirit)	1
4. Yaŋ guandɔŋ (cow of the grandfather)	1
5. Yaŋ mandɔŋ (cow of the grandmother)	1
6. Yaŋ guanleenä kɛnɛ thäkdɛ (cow of paternal uncle & bull of the girl)	2
7. Thak guande kene thak daman nya	2
8. Yaŋ wayä (cow of the paternal aunt)	1
9. Dɛi dɔaŋni kui guandɛ (calves of grandparents of father)	2

10. Ruedh dɔaŋni kui guandɛ (heifers for grandparents)   2
11. Ruath yiɣni (small ox for the master of ceremonies)   1

Total   17

II. Maternal Uncles. Pek Närä (pek gɔal).

1. Yaŋ guandɔŋ kɛnɛ yaŋ mandɔŋ (cows for the grandfather and mother)   2
2. Yaŋ Närä kɛnɛ thäkdɛ (cow for the uncle and a bull)   2
3. Yaŋ Manleenä (cow of the aunt)   1
4. Dɛi dɔaŋni kui Närä (calves for grandparents)   2
5. Ruedh dɔaŋni kui Närä (small oxen of grandparents)   2

Total: 9

Summary 17 + 9 = **26 cows**

Appendix 2B

Medium Form of Marriage Settlement No. 2 (Kuen Nuäärä min te däär)

	Total
I. <u>Father's Side (Pek Guandɛ)</u>	
1. Yaŋ guandɛ kɛnɛ yaŋ kuɔdhdɛ (cow of the father and a bull for his God)	2
2. Yaŋ Mandɛ kɛnɛ yaŋ kuɔdhdɛ (Cow for the mother and a bull for her God)	2
3. Yaŋ Jɔak Pukä kɛnɛ yaŋ Bilä (Cow for the spirit and another for God of the heavens)	2
4. Yaŋ guandɔŋ kɛnɛ yaŋ mandɔŋ	2
5. Yaŋ guanleenä kɛnɛ thäkdɛ	9
6. Yaŋ wayä kɛnɛ yaŋ tɔŋni mandɛ	2
7. Dɛi dɔaŋni kui guandɛ	2
8. Ruedh dɔaŋni kui guandɛ	2
9. Ruath yiɣni	1
10. Thäk guandɛ kɛnɛ däman nyal	2
Total:	19

II. Pek Närä.   Total
1. Yaŋ guandɔŋ kɛnɛ yaŋ mandɛ   2
2. Yaŋ Närä kɛnɛ thäkdɛ   2
3. Yaŋ Manleenä   1
4. Dɛi dɔaŋni kui närä   2
5. Ruedh dɔaŋni kui närä   2

Total: 9

Summary Pek guandɛ + Pek Närä 19 + 9 = **28 cows**

Appendix 2C
Long form of Marriage Settlement No. 3
(Kuen Nuäärä min bärien)

I. Pek Guandɛ   Total
1. Yaŋ guandɛ kɛ dɔw kɛnɛ yaŋ kuɔdhdɛ   3
2. Yaŋ mandɛ kɛ dɔw kɛnɛ yaŋ kuɔdhdɛ   3
3. Thäk guandɛ kɛnɛ däman nyal   2
4. Yaŋ wayä kɛnɛ yaŋ tɔŋni mandɛ   2
5. Yaŋ guandɔŋ kɛ yaŋ mandɔŋ kɛ dɛikiɛn   4
6. Yaŋ guanleenä kɛ dɔw kɛ thäk   3
7. Yaŋ Bilä kɛnɛ yaŋ jɔak pukä   2
8. Ruath yiɣni kiɛ thäk ŋuɔtni   1
9. Dɛi dɔaŋni pek guandɛ   2
10. Ruedh dɔaŋni   2

Total: 24

II. Pek Närä`
1. Yaŋ guandɔŋ kɛnɛ yaŋ mandɔŋ kɛ dɛi kiɛn   4
2. Yaŋ Närä kɛ dɔwdɛ kɛ thäkdɛ   3
3. Dɛi dɔaŋni pek Närä   2

4. Yaŋ Manleen` 1.   1
5. Ruedh dɔaŋni pek Närä 2.   2

Total   12

Summary: **Pek Guandɛ** = 24 cows.
                Pek Närä = 12 cows.

                Grand total = 36 cows.

Appendix 2D
Marriage Settlement No. 4 (Inflated)
(Kuen Nuäärä mi ca reph)

I. <u>Pek Guandɛ</u> Total
1. Dọdjic (yaŋ jiɛc) 1
2. Yaŋ guandɛ kɛnɛ dɔwdɛ kɛ thäk 3
3. Yaŋ kuɔdh guandɛ 1
4. Yaŋ Bilä 1
5. Yaŋ jɔak pukä 1
6. Yaŋ cọlwei 1
7. Yaŋ bɛag/purɛe/riay/galam etc. 1
8. Yaŋ mandɛ kɛnɛ dɔw 2
9. Yaŋ kuɔdh mandɛ 1
10. Yaŋ cak mandɛ 1
11. Yaŋ tɔŋni mandɛ 1
12. Thäk däman nyal 1
13. Thäk guanleenä 1
14. Yaŋ guanleenä 1
15. Yaŋ mandɔŋ guandɛ 1
16. Yaŋ guanleen kui luak 1
17. Yaŋ guandɔŋ 1

18. Yaŋ wayä	1
19. Yaŋ manleenä	1
20. Yaŋ mädhdɛ (friendship)	1
21. Dɛi dɔaŋni daŋ rɛu	2
22. Ruedh dɔaŋni daŋ rɛu	2
Total:	27

II. <u>Pek Närä</u>

1. Yaŋ mandɔŋ te dɔw	2
2. Yaŋ guandɔŋ	1
3. Yaŋ Närä	1
4. Thäk Närä	1
5. Dɛi dɔaŋni daŋ rɛu + Ruedh dɔaŋni daŋ rɛu	4
6. Ruath yiɣni	1
Total:	10

Grand total = Pek guandɛ + Pek Närä= 27+10 = 37 cows

Glossary

Some Nuäär terms have been tossed around in the text which might confuse the reader. The below are some explanations of the most important ones.

Luɔm nyal an expression of love by the youth is the first stage in wedding. It is an important step which the elders from both sides monitor remotely.

Paph Yiɣni or määdni tuaini, refers to the joint meeting of the spouse parents. *Paph* means to lay down. *Yiɣni* are the papyrus mats. So it is the laying down of the papyrus mats for the meeting. *Määdni* is lumping together. *Tuaai* are the leopard skins. Hence *määdni tuaini* is the lumping or joining together of the civet cat skins. This *paph yiɣni* or *määdni tuaini* is a serious visit to the marriage in regards to homicide, relations or minor issues and what can severe relations. Any successful outcome is followed with an announcement by the groom's father that, "I shall bring my rope home and engage the girl". *Bi guan gatä (wutä) we bä kandä noŋ bä cuɛc.*

Cuɛc is another form of *luɔm* except that the elders are the determinants. It is the driving to the bride's home of more cattle to concretise the marriage. At this stage the bride is considered a wife no matter whatever happens to her. When a girl under *cuɛc* is eloped, raped, or abducted, she is considered somebody's wife, because most of the marriage cattle had gone to the bride's people through the *luɔm* and *cuɛc*. Those that remained cannot prevent the wedding ceremony.

The betting of the bride-wealth payment ***tuɔc*** is done by the elders.

Buɔr is actually the completion of cattle pledging. *Buɔr ɛ lat yɔk*. The important part is the feasting.

Thuɔm **ghost** is someone who died unmarried. In disregard of marriage *thuɔm* refers to all the dead of long ago.

Jɔk is spirit.

Ciek cieŋ - *ciek* (wife), ***cieŋ*** (family- household). **Ciek cieŋ** refers to family/household wife.

Ciek tɛar - is wife of the feud (*tɛar*). This is a woman married from homicide wealth to continue the feud.

Tuac - the civet cat or leopard skin.

Tek in dorar (never ending) ever lasting life. Life that is everlasting.

Nyadhuɔri is supposed to be written *nyal* (girl) *dhuɔri* (of the tassels). This refers to a fresh girl that has the connotation of virginity i.e. not known to have ever been married, eloped nor impregnated.

Kɛa - second hand woman i.e. married and divorced, eloped and divorced or impregnated but not made a wife. When a *kɛa* is taken as temporary wife without payment she becomes a *luɔm*-concubine.

Kual nyal - eloping a girl. *Kual* generally means to steal.

Kuaruaŋ - disabled.

Cuɛay - twin (*cuɛaa*- twins).

Cam - left, left-handed.

Mɔy - child whose mother conceived without experiencing menustration.

Tor - monorchid (one -testicled male, human or animal).

Cɔr - blind.

Miŋ - deaf.

Duääny - crippled.

Pεac - captive.

Puth - purify.

Nuäär - contaminate.

Daw - heifer.

Dart - red mouth.

Wut - man.

Wuud - ostriche or manhood.

Mar - relation.

Nyaricädu - your age-mate's daughter. It is combination of three words: *Nyal* (daughter) *ric* (age-mate) *du* (your).

Däägh riyä - separation of generation. *Dääg* (separate or pull apart) *riy/ric* generation/mate.

Kɔɔr - a type of incest.

Cuŋ - rights (singular is *cuɔŋ*).

Gɔl - is the heap of smouldering cattle dung in the center of a byre and the hearth of ashes around it. Every *cieŋ* family must make one. In wider connotation *gɔl* is lineage.

Bibliography

Raymond C. Kelly, <u>The Nuer Conquest</u>, The University of Michigan Press, 1985.

Sharon E. Hutchinson, <u>Nuer Dillemas</u>, University of California Press, Berkeley, Los Angeles, London, 1996.

Mercy Amba Oduyoye & Musimbi R.A. Kanyoro (Edit.). <u>The Will to Arise</u>, Orbis Books, Maryknoll, NY. 10545, 1992. [Oduyoye/ Konyaro].

Paul G. Hierbert, <u>Cultural Anthropology</u>, Baker Book House, Grand Rapids, Michigan 49506, 1983.

Elmer S. Miller, <u>Introduction to Cultural Anthropology</u>, Englewood Cliffs, N.J. 1979.

Evans-Pritchard, E.E., <u>Kinship and Marriage among the Nuer</u>, Oxford University Press, Oxford 1951.

Nathan Glazer & Daniel P.Moynihan (edit). <u>Ethnicity:Theory and Experience</u>, Harvard University Press, Cambridge, Massachusetts and London, England, 1975.

Ladislov Holy, <u>Neighbours and Kinsmen,: A study of the Berti People of Darfur</u>, C. Hurst and Company, London 1974.

Parrinder, Geoffrey, <u>African Traditional Religion</u>, 3rd ed. London and New York: Harper and Row, 1976.

About the Author

James Mabor Gatkuoth Nyak Tɔaŋ Dọdh was born in Nyuɔŋ, Payinjiar county, Unity State, South Sudan. He is married and has children. He got educated in Ler Elementary, Obel Intermediate, American Commercial High School- Omdurman and then University of Khartoum- Faculty of Economic and Social Studies from which he graduated and obtained B.SC. Degree in Political Science, M.A. from African and Asian Studies Institute and Ph. D. from the main Faculty in 2011.

He served in Labour Department in the then Southern Region and was assigned to manage May Vocational Training Centre in Wau. In 1982 he was elected from Ler Geographical Constituency No. 45 to the 4th (the last) Southern Regional Assembly from which he was appointed Commissioner of Upper Nile Province (now split to Upper Nile and Unity states). After the collapse of Numeiri's regime, he was employed Director of Advocacy and Communication by the Sudan Council of Churches in April 1991 till March 1998. From March 1998 to August 2000 became Minister for Humanitarian Affairs in the Coordinating Council Government for South Sudan instituted by the peace treaty that Dr. Riek Machar brokered on 21.4.1997.

He likes reading and writing. Accordingly, he presented papers to local workshops, seminars, magazines, and an international conference. Apart from his academic requirements for postgraduate studies, he wrote a book- <u>Nuäär Social Rights and Obligations</u>, published in Uganda, October 2012. Forthcoming are:- (1) Reflection on the rise and collapse of the self-governing autonomy in Southern Sudan 1972-83. (2) The Genealogy of the Nuäär Liei Generation.

www.ingramcontent.com/pod-product-compliance
Lightning Source LLC
Chambersburg PA
CBHW030254010526
44107CB00053B/1712